Sexual Harassment in the Workplace

Create a Better Workplace for Everyone

Third Edition

Juliana Lightle, Ph.D.
and Elizabeth H. Doucet, Esq.

Viva Books
New Delhi | Mumbai | Chennai | Kolkata
Bengaluru | Hyderabad | Kochi | Guwahati

First Indian Edition 2011

VIVA BOOKS PRIVATE LIMITED

- 4737/23 Ansari Road, Daryaganj, New Delhi 110 002
  E-mail: vivadelhi@vivagroupindia.net, Tel. 42242200
- 76, Service Industries, Shirvane, Sector 1, Nerul, Navi Mumbai 400 706
  E-mail: vivamumbai@vivagroupindia.net, Tel. 27721273, 27721274
- Jamals Fazal Chambers, 26 Greams Road, Chennai 600 006
  E-mail: vivachennai@vivagroupindia.net, Tel. 28290304, 28294241
- B-103, Jindal Towers, 21/1A/3 Darga Road, Kolkata 700 017
  E-mail: vivakolkata@vivagroupindia.net, Tel. 22836381, 22816713
- 7, Sovereign Park Apartments, 56-58, K. R. Road, Basavanagudi, Bengaluru 560 004
  E-mail: vivabangalore@vivagroupindia.net, Tel. 26607409, 26607410
- 101-102 Mughal Marc Aptt., 3-4-637 to 641, Narayanguda, Hyderabad 500 029
  E-mail: vivahyderabad@vivagroupindia.net, Tel. 27564481, 27564482
- First Floor, Beevi Towers, SRM Road, Kaloor, Kochi 682 018, Kerala
  E-mail: vivakochi@vivagroupindia.net, Tel: 0484-2403055, 2403056
- 232, GNB Road, Beside UCO Bank, Silpukhuri, Guwahati 781 003
  E-mail: vivaguwahati@vivagroupindia.net, Tel: 0361-2666386

www.vivagroupindia.com

Published by arrangement with

Axzo Press, LLC
562, Willow Brook Office Park
Fairport, New York 14450

ISBN : 978-81-309-1845-7

Published by Vinod Vasishtha for Viva Books Private Limited, 4737/23, Ansari Road, Daryaganj, New Delhi - 110 002. Printed and bound by Raj Press, R-3, Inderpuri, New Delhi - 110 012.

Table of Contents

About the Authors

Elizabeth Doucet has been practicing law for 34 years in New York, Louisiana, and Ohio. She was an attorney with the Equal Employment Opportunity Commission in Washington, D.C., and New Orleans, and she was regional attorney of the New Orleans office for several years. For the past 25 years, she has been concentrating her practice in employment law, having worked for a labor law firm in New York and California, and later for a national retailer.

Ms. Doucet graduated from Temple University in Philadelphia with a degree in journalism and from Loyola University New Orleans College of Law. Before attending law school, she was a reporter for United Press International in Newark, New Jersey, and South Vietnam.

Ms. Doucet has lectured extensively on employment law, specifically sexual harassment. She now resides in Louisiana while working on three books.

Juliana Lightle's career history includes eight years in higher education administration and 15 years in corporate human resources, including management positions in affirmative action and labor relations. She has published technical articles on the shortage of engineers and scientists and has served as an expert witness in sexual harassment cases.

Ms. Lightle received her Ph.D. in counseling and labor and human resources from Ohio State University. She now consults, writes, teaches high school, and raises horses in Texas.

Preface

All of us want to work in a safe, secure, enjoyable, and profitable environment. We want to produce good work and contribute to the success of our workplace, wherever that is.

But sexual harassment, or harassment of any kind, destroys the enjoyment of the workplace for everyone. Sexual harassment continues to interfere with workplace satisfaction and productivity for a substantial number of men and women.

When we first wrote *Sexual Harassment in the Workplace* in 1992, the courts in the United States had just started to look at this issue. Since 1992, the courts, including the U.S. Supreme Court, have continued to address the issue of sexual harassment and to define issues related to it. Can only a woman be sexually harassed? Does the harasser have to be a co-worker or a member of the opposite sex for a court to find that the line has been crossed? What are the consequences of an organization's not having legal assistance when it is charged with sexual harassment?

In preparing this revision of *Sexual Harassment in the Workplace*, we realized that we had initially written a book with a new vision of the workplace. The courts have embraced that vision, adopting much of what we and other human resources professionals recommended in an attempt to eliminate harassment in the workplace. The courts have also acknowledged the responsibility of employers to train their supervisors and managers. Some states, such as California, have mandated sexual harassment training for all supervisory personnel.

Unfortunately, recent statistics show that sexual harassment remains a problem. We continue to believe that sexual harassment can be eliminated without taking the fun out of the workplace. All organizations can set a tone that creates trust, security, achievement, and a desire for excellence.

As we review the changes in the laws, you will be able to look at your own attitudes and beliefs about others in the workplace and about differences among the people with whom you work. You will learn how you can relate to different individuals more effectively and what steps employers must take to protect their resources, their employees, and their finances from sexual harassment.

This book looks at sexual harassment from two perspectives:

- **Prevention** — How to create a positive workplace
- **The legal aspects** — What the courts have said and how that affects what to do before and after a complaint is filed

The exercises in this book are based on our experience as human resources professionals and on our observations of the effective handling of complaints and lawsuits. We encourage you to complete these exercises. They will cause you to examine your own behaviors and perhaps reevaluate some possibly inappropriate or negative behaviors. We believe the workplace can be free of harassing, ineffectual, and divisive behaviors and remain open, fun, and productive.

Elizabeth H. Doucet

Juliana Lightle

Limits of Liability and Disclaimer of Warranty

The author and publisher of this book have used their best efforts in the preparation of this book and make no warranty of any kind, expressed or implied, with regard to the instructions and suggestions contained in this book.

Learning Objectives

Complete this book, and you'll know how to:

1) Understand the many forms of sexual harassment and the effects it can have on the workplace
2) Learn the legal definition of sexual harassment and how the issue is being handled in the courts
3) Implement a sexual harassment policy and harassment-prevention training in the workplace
4) Investigate and resolve sexual harassment complaints that may arise
5) Minimize legal problems when accusers seek assistance from government agencies and the courts
6) Address unwelcome behavior and create a positive, supportive workplace

About the Viva-Crisp 50-Minute Series

The Viva-Crisp 50-Minute Series was designed to cover critical business and professional development topics in the shortest possible time. Our easy-to-read, easy-to-understand format can be used for self-study or for classroom training. With a wealth of hands-on exercises, the 50-Minute books keep you engaged and help you retain critical skills.

What You Need to Know

We designed the Viva-Crisp 50-Minute Series to be as self-explanatory as possible. But there are a few things you should know before you begin the book.

Exercises

Exercises look like this:

EXERCISE TITLE

Questions and other information would be here.

Keep a pencil handy. Any time you see an exercise, you should try to complete it. If the exercise has specific answers, an answer key will be provided in the appendix. (Some exercises ask you to think about your own opinions or situation; these types of exercises will not have answer keys.)

Forms

A heading like this means that the rest of the page is a form:

FORMHEAD

Forms are meant to be reusable. You might want to make a photocopy of a form before you fill it out, so that you can use it again later.

A Note to Instructors

We've tried to make the Viva-Crisp 50-Minute Series books as useful as possible as classroom training manuals. Here are some of the features we provide for instructors:

- PowerPoint presentations
- Answer keys
- Assessments
- Customization

PowerPoint Presentations

You can download a PowerPoint presentation for this book from our Web site at www.CrispSeries.com.

Answer keys

If an exercise has specific answers, an answer key will be provided in the appendix. (Some exercises ask you to think about your own opinions or situation; these types of exercises will not have answer keys.)

Assessments

For each 50-Minute Series book, we have developed a 35- to 50-item assessment. The assessment for this book is available at www.CrispSeries.com. *Assessments should not be used in any employee-selection process.*

PART 1

Understanding Sexual Harassment in the Workplace

In this part:

- Origins of Workplace Sexual Harassment
- The Shifting Balance of Power Between the Sexes
- How Prevalent Is Sexual Harassment?
- Who Are the Victims and Who Are the Accused?
- Effects of Societal Stereotypes
- Effects on Individuals and the Workplace

TEST YOUR KNOWLEDGE OF SEXUAL HARASSMENT

Before beginning this book, check your current knowledge of sexual harassment. Check (✓) **T** for True and **F** for False.

	T	F
1. Sexual harassment concerns only women who are employed.	❑	❑
2. An organization that has a policy prohibiting sexual harassment in the workplace, even if not well publicized, will be insulated from charges and lawsuits alleging sexual harassment.	❑	❑
3. The only way an organization and its managers can ensure that there are no sexual harassment complaints is to limit relationships among employees.	❑	❑
4. The courts have ruled that in investigating claims of sexual harassment, the standard to be applied is that of the reasonable woman.	❑	❑
5. Most instances of sexual harassment involve requests for sexual favors.	❑	❑
6. Sexual harassment policies must include all employees, even those who are puritanical or prudish.	❑	❑
7. If found guilty of sexual harassment, an employee may be individually liable to the harassed employee and may be ordered by the court to pay out-of-pocket expenses not reimbursable by the employer.	❑	❑
8. Under the concept of "ugly" discrimination, employees can bring complaints or file lawsuits where employment decisions are based on an employee's submitting to sexual harassment and an "ugly" employee's not being offered the opportunity to submit to such harassment.	❑	❑
9. Most charges or complaints of sexual harassment are made by troublemakers, since harassment is not a problem in all workplaces.	❑	❑
10. Sexual harassment is going to occur, regardless of what employers or their employees do to avoid it.	❑	❑

Correct responses to these questions are in the Appendix. But do not look now. Wait until you have completed the book, and then test your knowledge again.

Origins of Workplace Sexual Harassment

Judging from historical accounts, sexual harassment has always occurred, but there was no label for such behavior. Attitudes began to shift when women gained more equality in the workplace.

Changing Roles Between Men and Women

The industrial revolution brought about changes in the traditional roles of men and women that greatly increased gender specialization and created a new kind of workplace in the Western world. Men and women no longer worked together on the farm or in the family trade. The role of each sex became more specialized.

This job specialization continued to increase. As people continued to move to the cities, the need for economic security also increased. People were no longer self-sufficient. Thus, the roles for males and females became increasingly narrowly defined, and for the vast majority of people, very comfortable. Everyone knew exactly what was expected and how to behave. There was little, if any, ambiguity.

The stereotypical roles of men and women became more extreme. Women who worked outside the home usually did so at specific kinds of jobs, mostly with other women. They held "appropriate" jobs, in keeping with the stereotypes. Women among the middle and upper classes became the "weaker sex." Men were expected to be strong and to work to support the women and children. Thus, women became increasingly dependent. This situation gave men much greater power.

Since the power balance favored men, they felt free to engage in behaviors that nowadays would be labeled sexual harassment. And women's lack of power meant they had little choice but to accept it. Harassment occurred because organizations and managers allowed it to occur. In some cases, they even set a tone that encouraged it.

That all began to change as more and more women joined the workforce and increasingly moved into jobs that were traditionally held by males.

The Shifting Balance of Power Between the Sexes

The balance of power in the workplace has changed dramatically in the past several decades. And change continues to accelerate. The struggle for power and position seems endless. Sexual harassment is one result of this struggle.

Men who felt secure with the old ways did not expect to have to compete with women. Now the old behavior models no longer work. This difficulty is compounded because generally accepted, pervasive rules of behavior keep evolving, as exemplified by the following questions:

- Should men hold doors open for women?
- Who pays the check when men and women at work have lunch together?
- Who lifts heavy boxes that need to be moved to the department storeroom?
- Can the good old jokes men used to tell each other at meetings be told in front of women?

Flight or Fight—or Adapt

Fear and uncertainty lead to polarizing hostility. Typical reactions are flight or fight. Neither works; both are costly for individuals and those around them.

When a male commits harassment against a female, it may be a response to real or imagined loss of power. When committed by a woman against a man, it may be an expression of retaliation or a "flexing" of the "new" power.

In the face of these workplace changes, individuals have two choices:

- Struggle more intensely
- Adapt

Some people cannot adapt. Some will use any means to compete, rather than pursue personal and professional growth. Growth—change—is difficult, tedious, and exhausting.

How do you deal with change? Write your answer in the space below.

____

____

____

____

____

"Mixed Company" at Work

How well are you adapting to the shifting balance of power between men and women in the workplace? To get some insights, describe how you deal with others at work, with men and with women. Ask yourself these questions and write your responses on the lines below:

- Do you respect individuality?
- Do you expect to be treated first as an individual and second as a woman or man—or vice versa?
- Are you supportive of others, regardless of their gender?

Have you ever made a business decision based on the gender of an individual, how you felt about the person sexually, or the person's sexual orientation?

____

____

Have you ever deliberately flirted at work? If so, what were the circumstances and why did you do it?

____

____

Do you wear clothes, cologne, or makeup to enhance, exploit, or subdue your masculinity or femininity ?

____

If this is the first time you have thought about these questions, what is your response to them? Surprise, discomfort, what?

____

How Prevalent Is Sexual Harassment?

Sexual harassment has been part of the workplace for many years, accepted as part of the atmosphere or terms and conditions of employment. A variety of surveys have attempted to measure the extent of harassment in the workplace, from government to corporate environments.

In 1981, *Redbook* magazine interviewed 140,000 men and women about sexual harassment. Their findings revealed that 80% of those interviewed believed they had been sexually harassed. In all studies, no less than 40% of women reported harassment, and as many as 45% of men reported it, when admiring sexual comments were included as harassment.

In their *Guide to Affirmative Action*, Pamela Conrad and Robert Maddux cite an Illinois Task Force study, which found that:

- 90% of all women surveyed think sexual harassment is a problem
- 70% of all working women surveyed believe they have been harassed at one time or another

Of those who felt they had been harassed:

- 52% had been subjected to sexual remarks or teasing
- 42% had been the target of suggestive looks or leers
- 26% had experienced subtle hints or pressure
- 25% had been physically touched against their will or grabbed
- 20% had been propositioned
- 14% had been repeatedly pressured to engage in a personal relationship
- 9% reported other miscellaneous forms of unwanted sexual attention
- 2% experienced forms of coercive rape

Has the Prevalence Changed?

Have these percentages changed in the last 20 to 25 years? Not really. Although the number of cases of men harassing women has shown a small decrease, the biggest changes have been an increase in men willing to report female bosses who harass and a greater incidence of same-sex harassment, primarily men against men, being reported.

In a federal government study, the number of both men and women who said they had been harassed showed little change over time. Only about 6% said they had reported the harassment.

Joan Kennedy Taylor, author of *What to Do When You Don't Want to Call the Cops*, emphasizes that, compared with the millions of workers, a mere 15,000 complaints are filed overall annually. Few actually go to trial because of out-of-court settlements, cases being dropped, and no-merit findings. Given these statistics, why bother with training and addressing sexual harassment concerns? Because sexual harassment—all harassment, in fact—poisons the workplace.

YOUR EXPERIENCES WITH SEXUAL HARASSMENT

Almost everyone either has experienced harassment personally or knows someone who has. If you have not experienced harassment and do not believe it is prevalent, ask colleagues or friends about their experience. Use the space below to describe such an experience, either yours or someone else's. Include where it occurred and what form the harassment took.

____

____

____

____

____

What about the situation caused you to see it as harassment? How did you feel? NOTE: If you are using a friend's or colleague's experience, do you view it differently than he or she did? How? Why?

____

____

____

____

Who Are the Victims and Who Are the Accused?

Nearly all females have at one time or another heard offensive jokes, catcalls, and whistles when on the street. These behaviors often occur outside the workplace and are not related to work in any way. Women learn to deal with these forms of harassment as they grow up, usually by simply ignoring them. But what about harassment at work or at school?

Recent history has shown that sexual harassment does not occur only in nightclubs or places of entertainment or corporate offices. No work environment—including schools, law offices, government agencies, and religious institutions—is free from the potential for sexual harassment. There is no special modus operandi, race, sex, or age for accused sexual harassers. They come from all walks of life, all ages, and both sexes.

The Role of Power Disparity

In 1991, at two Minnesota high schools, two girls sued their high schools when the schools failed to respond to harassment complaints. Both of these incidents were cases of student-to-student harassment, but female college students also report high percentages of harassment from male professors. Harassed college students rarely report this abuse because they fear that professors will retaliate by giving them poor grades and substandard job recommendations.

Indeed, although the victim of sexual harassment and the person accused might be peers, more often the victim is in a position of lesser power than the accused. The classic cases are managers or supervisors using their formal power to harass: "If you do not comply, I will [fire you, not hire you, not promote you…]." This situation is referred to as *quid pro quo*, or something given or received for something else. Harassment can also occur between customers or clients and providers.

The Role of Gender Ratio

One federal study (Department of Defense) indicates that the individuals most likely to experience harassment are those who work in an environment where most, if not all, of their peers are the opposite sex and those who are exclusively supervised by members of the opposite sex. Examples include female construction workers and welders and female surgeons.

In *Men and Women of the Corporation*, Rosabeth Moss Kanter noted that populations in a work environment relate differently depending on their proportions. Many sex-role problems, and consequently sexual harassment, diminish when gender ratio is more balanced.

Effects of Societal Stereotypes

None of us lives and works in an objective world, and individuals do not behave objectively. Each person's biases about men and women, attractiveness and unattractiveness, and who is likely to harass whom, all creep into the workplace, no matter how hard individuals try to be objective.

Studies on sexual harassment have demonstrated that societal stereotypes affect outcomes. In one study (J.G. Wayne, C.M. Riordam, and K.M. Thomas, "Is All Sexual Harassment Viewed the Same? Mock Juror Decisions in Same and Cross-Cases," *Journal of Applied Psychology* 86 (2001): 176–187), women who harass men were more likely to be found guilty than were men who harass women, and same-sex cases were the most likely to result in a guilty verdict.

In another study (J.H. Golden III, C.H. Johnson, and R.H. Lopez, "Sexual Harassment in the Workplace: Exploring the Effects of Attractiveness on Perception of Harassment," *Sex Roles* 45 (2001): 767–784), attractiveness of both men and women greatly affected the way that harassment was viewed. The more attractive the man, the less likely that he was viewed as a harasser. The more attractive the woman, the more likely she was seen as harassed, especially if the man was not seen as attractive.

Cultural Beliefs about Gender and Behavior

The ways in which people are brought up, including their cultural beliefs about women and men, greatly affect their behavior. Harassment is linked to prejudice and sexist attitudes. Men who were raised to have macho attitudes are inclined to treat female colleagues differently than are men who were brought up to see women as equals.

Similarly, women raised to believe that the female's main role is to please men may have a more difficult time appropriately asserting themselves than will women raised to see themselves as equal to men. Confusion may also result from different cultures' views about what is appropriate and acceptable behavior at work.

In *Sex and the Workplace*, Barbara Gutek reports on a study indicating that the majority of men think women are flattered by sexual innuendo and overtures at work. In fact, women are not. The vast majority of women want to be valued for their work, period. Men are rarely, if ever, seen as a decorative asset. Women do not want to be decorative assets, either. They want to be taken seriously and valued for the work they do.

The point of citing these studies is to emphasize that in order to be the most effective and productive they can be at work, individuals need to know their own biases and understand how they are affected by them.

EXPLORING GENDER STEREOTYPES

Below is a list of words often used to describe individuals. Beside each word, place an F if that description is stereotypically female or an M if it describes a male stereotype:

_____ Wishy-washy
_____ Strong
_____ Passive
_____ Objective
_____ Excitable
_____ Moody
_____ Protective
_____ Achiever
_____ Subjective
_____ Cheerful
_____ Soft-spoken
_____ Unreliable
_____ Competitive

_____ Dependent
_____ Doer
_____ Assertive
_____ Cooperative
_____ Competent
_____ Important
_____ Fearful
_____ Risk taker
_____ Nice
_____ Weak
_____ Follower
_____ Gentle
_____ Consistent

_____ Cautious
_____ Kind
_____ Leader
_____ Powerful
_____ Brave
_____ Stoical
_____ Unemotional
_____ Decisive
_____ Warm
_____ Flexible
_____ Emotional
_____ Aggressive

Everyone is familiar with these stereotypes. Even if they no longer apply in most situations, stereotypes continue to affect behavior, the way we describe one another, and our ways of interrelating.

Now go back through the list and check (✓) every word that applies to you. Most likely you will find that you have some combination of both male and female stereotypical traits. How do you feel when someone attributes the stereotype for your sex to you?

____

____

____

Everyone has some beliefs based on stereotypes. The problem comes from applying them to make inaccurate and unfair comparisons or to judge others.

Effects on Individuals and the Workplace

Whatever the cause, sexual harassment is serious and costly with dire monetary, physical, and psychological consequences. Sexual harassment can affect the entire life of an organization and its members. Sexual harassment, in all its forms, is damaging to the workplace. It affects both the individuals harassed and the persons accused, who may be innocent.

It can go even further than that. It can generate costly lawsuits, unfavorable publicity, and the invasion of privacy.

List below the effects you believe sexual harassment has on:

The Victim

____

____

The Accused

____

____

The Organization

____

____

Monetary Costs Add Up

Sexual harassment can affect the bottom line of the employer, whether it's a school, corporation, or governmental entity, as well as reach into the pocketbooks of supervisors, managers, and co-workers.

If a person is found to have sexually harassed another individual, the courts might not permit the harasser's employer to pay the court costs, attorney's fees, or damages assessed against them. In a number of cases, the courts have ordered individuals who have been found guilty of harassment to pay these costs themselves.

In a government study of sexual harassment within the federal government in the early 1980s, findings showed that lost time and productivity from sexual harassment cost the government $188.7 million over a two-year period. Forty-two percent of the women and 14% of the men stated that they had experienced harassment. When the study was repeated five years later, those percentages had not decreased, and costs had increased to $267 million. A more current federal government study indicates an even higher cost, $327 million. Sexual harassment is not cheap! No organization can afford it.

How Would You Define Sexual Harassment?

Sexual harassment is not easy to define. Not all agencies or courts define it in the same way. Like all illegal acts of discrimination, it is not always clear and it is often a very personal matter, as viewed by the individual affected.

How would you define it? Write your definition below.

____

____

Would your definition be different if you were of the opposite sex?
Why or why not?

____

____

Would you define sexual harassment differently if you were a parent?
Why or why not?

____

____

Compare your answers on this self-test with the authors' responses in the Appendix.

WHAT ACTIONS CONSTITUTE SEXUAL HARASSMENT?

Now test your knowledge and biases with this true/false quiz. Check (✓) T for true or F for false. You may find some of these statements difficult to respond to.

	T	F
1. Only physical acts by one employee against another constitutes sexual harassment.	❑	❑
2. A suggestive or sexist cartoon hanging over an employee's desk constitutes sexual harassment.	❑	❑
3. Ignoring another employee constitutes sexual harassment.	❑	❑
4. Actions of a sexual nature by non-employees are sexual harassment.	❑	❑
5. Staring at an employee is not sexual harassment.	❑	❑
6. Dirty jokes or jokes with sexual innuendoes are not sexual harassment.	❑	❑
7. Unwelcome touching of one employee by another would not be considered sexual harassment.	❑	❑
8. The promotion of a willing participant in an office romance is not sexual harassment.	❑	❑
9. Failure to promote an employee because he or she will not date you is sexual harassment.	❑	❑
10. Inviting a subordinate to go out on a date, even though the person has refused to go out with you in the past, is sexual harassment.	❑	❑

Compare your answers on this self-test with the authors' responses in the Appendix.

Part Summary

- Sexual harassment has always occurred, but attitudes about it began to shift when women gained more equality in the workplace.
- Sexual harassment is one result of the struggle for power and position between men and women in the workplace.
- Over the years, the number of cases of men harassing women has decreased slightly, but there's also been an increase in the number of men willing to report being harassed by female bosses and by other men.
- Harassment is linked to prejudice and sexist attitudes. Our cultural beliefs about women and men greatly affect our behavior.
- Whatever the cause, sexual harassment is serious and costly with dire monetary, physical, and psychological consequences. Sexual harassment can affect the entire life of an organization and its members.

"Who threw that heel?"

PART 2

Defining Sexual Harassment Under the Law

In this part:

- The EEOC Addresses Sexual Harassment
- Sexual Harassment and the Courts
- What Actions Are Sexual Harassment?
- Vicarious Employer Liability
- Potential Costs of Legal Defense and Damages
- Sexual Harassment vs. Sex Discrimination

The EEOC Addresses Sexual Harassment

Although the Civil Rights Act of 1964 (Title VII) guaranteed certain rights for all people, the concept of sexual harassment as a legal claim is relatively new.

The concept was first addressed in 1980 by the courts and the Equal Employment Opportunity Commission (EEOC), the U.S. federal agency that is responsible for enforcing anti-discrimination laws. In 1980, the EEOC issued *Guidelines on Sexual Harassment in the Workplace*. Although guidelines are not law, the U.S. Supreme Court has said the EEOC Guidelines should be accorded the same weight as laws.

These EEOC Guidelines describe *sexual harassment* as:

> Unwelcome sexual advances, requests for sexual favors, and other verbal or physical conduct of a sexual nature, when:
>
> a) Submission to such conduct is made explicitly or implicitly a term or condition of an individual's employment.
>
> b) Submission to or rejection of such conduct by an individual is used as the basis for employment decisions affecting the individual.
>
> c) Such conduct has the purpose or effect of unreasonably interfering with an individual's work performance or creating an intimidating, hostile, or offensive working environment.

Anyone in the workplace can be sexually harassed. Similarly, anyone in the workplace and even persons not employed by the organization can be accused of and be liable for acts of sexual harassment.

In its guidelines, the EEOC stated that the best way for an employer to deal with sexual harassment is to take all necessary steps to prevent it, including:

- Proactively raising the subject
- Expressing strong disapproval
- Developing appropriate sanctions
- Informing employees of their rights to raise the issue
- Developing methods to make sure that all employees are sensitive to the issue

The EEOC Guidelines are spelled out on the following page.

EEOC Guidelines

Sec. 1604.11 Sexual Harassment

(a) Harassment on the basis of sex is a violation of Sec. 703 of Title VII. Unwelcome sexual advances, requests for sexual favors, and other verbal or physical conduct of a sexual nature constitute sexual harassment when (1) submission to such conduct is made either explicitly or implicitly a term or condition of an individual's employment, (2) submission to or rejection of such conduct by an individual is used as the basis for employment decisions affecting such individual, or (3) such conduct has the purpose or effect of unreasonably interfering with an individual's work performance or creating an intimidating, hostile, or offensive working environment.

(b) In determining whether alleged conduct constitutes sexual harassment, the Commission will look at the record as a whole and the totality of the circumstances, such as the nature of the sexual advances and the context in which the alleged incidents occurred. The determination of the legality of a particular action will be made from the facts, on a case-by-case basis.

(c) [Vicarious Employer Liability for Unlawful Harassment by Supervisors is explained later in this part of the book.]

(d) With respect to conduct between fellow employees, an employer is responsible for acts of sexual harassment in the workplace where the employer (or its agents or supervisory employees) knows or should have known of the conduct, unless it can show that it took immediate and appropriate corrective action.

(e) An employer may also be responsible for the acts of non-employees, with respect to sexual harassment of employees in the workplace, where the employer (or its agents or supervisory employees) knows or should have known of the conduct and fails to take immediate and appropriate corrective action. In reviewing these cases the Commission will consider the extent of the employer's control and any other legal responsibility which the employer may have with respect to the conduct of such non-employees.

(f) Prevention is the best tool for the elimination of sexual harassment. An employer should take all steps necessary to prevent sexual harassment from occurring, such as affirmatively raising the subject, expressing strong disapproval, developing appropriate sanctions, informing employees of their right to raise and how to raise the issue of harassment under Title VII, and developing methods to sensitize all concerned.

(g) Other related practices: Where employment opportunities or benefits are granted because of an individual's submission to the employer's requests for sexual favors, the employer may be held liable for unlawful sex discrimination against other persons who were qualified for but denied that employment opportunity or benefit.

Sexual Harassment and the Courts

Since the EEOC issued its guidelines, more and more courts, from the lowest to the highest, have struggled with issues related to sexual harassment. Since the late 1980s, the courts in the United States have taken an aggressive role in trying to eliminate sexual harassment in the workplace.

Step by step, the courts have dealt with all of the issues addressed in the EEOC Guidelines. First the U.S. Supreme Court recognized the concept of sexual harassment and recognized that a hostile work environment could constitute sexual harassment.

More recently, the Supreme Court established a two-part test for employers who are defending sexual harassment lawsuits. Under this test, an employer would be liable for the harassment by one of its supervisors even if the employer had no knowledge of the action and the employee suffers what is called *tangible employment action*.

But an employer could demonstrate that it "exercised reasonable care" and acted promptly when advised of "sexually harassing behavior" if there was no tangible employment action and "the employee failed to take advantage of any preventive or corrective opportunities provided by the employer."

"Is it chauvinistic to ask 'which floor'?"

Court Rulings on Sexual Harassment in the Workplace

Various courts have found the existence of sexual harassment in the following situations:

- When a male supervisor told a female subordinate that her continued success and advancement at the organization depended on her agreeing to his sexual demands, the court found this to be a *condition of employment* within the meaning of the civil rights laws.
- An employer violated Title VII when one of its male supervisors terminated a female employee in retaliation for her refusing to submit to his sexual advances.
- An employee was sexually harassed in violation of Title VII when she was forced to work in an atmosphere replete with intimidation and offensive comments of a sexual nature.
- An employee was sexually harassed with regard to the terms and conditions of her employment when her supervisors sexually harassed her without her department director's intervening. The court said the employee was not required to show that she resisted the harassment and that she lost or was denied tangible job benefits.
- Homosexual advances by a male supervisor toward a male employee are prohibited by Title VII and are sexual harassment.
- The Supreme Court has also stated that employees forced to quit their jobs because they could not endure sexual harassment could sue their former employers.

What Actions Are Sexual Harassment?

The different forms of sexual harassment lie on a sexual exploitation continuum:

Increasing Physical Violence

verbal/visual harassment ⇨ physical harassment ⇨ rape ⇨ rape/murder

Typical Forms of Harassment

Verbal/Visual	Physical
▶ Risqué jokes ▶ Off-color remarks ▶ Leers ▶ Unwanted propositions ▶ Threats ▶ Passes ▶ Suggestive, violent, or sexual photographs ▶ Pinups, cartoons ▶ Unwanted sexual compliments ▶ Repeated requests for dates ▶ Repeated requests for sexual favors ▶ Excessive flirting ▶ Wearing revealing attire ▶ Staring	▶ Unwanted touching on any part of the body ▶ Touching of breast and hips ▶ Unwanted brushing against another's body ▶ Standing too close ▶ Excessive "lengthy" handshakes ▶ Physical attack

Harassment may take the form of a risqué joke or a more aggressive form, such as repeated inappropriate touching of another's body. Whether intentional or not, all sexual harassment is aggression against another person's body or psyche, using sex as the weapon.

Vicarious Employer Liability

The EEOC Guidelines on Sexual Harassment previously had set out the standard for an employer to be found liable under the theory of vicarious liability. This is the liability that a supervisory party, such as an employer, bears for the conduct of an associate or subordinate (*Black's Law Dictionary*), even if the organization did not know about the harassment.

Supreme Court Establishes the Standard

In 1998, when it ruled on two cases—Burlington Industries Inc. v Ellerth, 118 S.Ct. 2257, and Faragher v City of Boca Raton, 118 S.Ct. 2275—the U.S. Supreme Court for the first time established the standard of liability in sexual harassment cases in which there was an issue of vicarious liability.

As explained by the Enforcement Guidance directive, the standard of liability is premised on two principles: (1) An employer is responsible for the acts of its supervisors; and (2) employers should be encouraged to prevent harassment, and employees should be encouraged to avoid or limit the harm from harassment.

As a result, the Supreme Court held that an employer is always liable for a supervisor's harassment if it results in a tangible employment action. If the supervisor's actions do not result in a tangible employment action, however, the employer may be able to avoid liability or limit the damages assessed against it by raising what is called an *affirmative defense*. The affirmative defense must show that the employer exercised reasonable care to prevent harassing behavior and promptly corrected any harassing behavior, and must show that the employee unreasonably failed to take advantage of any preventive or corrective opportunities provided by the employer or to otherwise avoid harm.

EEOC Guidelines Amended

As a result of these two cases, the EEOC Guidelines were amended and the EEOC issued a 26-page directive titled *Enforcement Guidance on Vicarious Employer Liability for Unlawful Harassment by Supervisors*. The entire Enforcement Guidance directive is available at the Web site of the EEOC (www.eeoc.gov).

The directive also explains who qualifies as a *supervisor* for purposes of Title VII of the Civil Rights Act of 1964, as amended. Although the coverage of state statutes may vary, most state anti-discrimination statutes apply the EEOC definition of supervisor. For example, the newly enacted California law that requires training for supervisors every two years specifically states that for purposes of the training mandate, only employers with 50 or more employees are required to provide the training.

Potential Costs of Legal Defense and Damages

Organizations are best served by creating an atmosphere in which individuals feel comfortable addressing the complaint to the appropriate internal staff. But if the individual who has been sexually harassed seeks outside legal counsel, then that person will have to pay for that counsel, unless the attorney takes the case on a contingency basis. In such a case, the legal counsel obviously has a huge stake in proving the case against the organization.

Potential for Additional Damages

The organization—the defendant—of course has to pay for its own legal counsel. But it may have to pay much more if the person raising the claim wins and the court requires the defendant to pay the legal fees and court costs of the injured party.

The court may award additional damages for emotional distress and the like, in which case the amounts can be huge. Under recent cases, the courts have awarded punitive damages.

A 1991 amendment to the federal civil rights laws allows courts to award compensatory and punitive damages in discrimination cases in which there are no additional claims, as in claims for breach of contract, emotional distress, or other personal injury claims. Awards made possible by this amendment can be substantially higher than losses in a typical sex discrimination case—as high as $300,000 for punitive damages alone—against an organization with 500 or more employees. The price tag for a finding of discrimination against an organization with fewer than 100 employees may go as high as $50,000.

In one case, an employee who had been sexually harassed by her supervisor was awarded $50,000 for emotional distress. Another employee was awarded $975,000 in punitive damages when a jury found that the president of the company had forced the employee to have sex with him.

A 1998 settlement between 350 women and Mitsubishi reached $34 million. It did not help that 15 women, who continued to work there after the initial complaint in 1996, suffered death threats as well as other adverse work situations.

Potential for Individual Legal Liability

Some harassed individuals have sued their harassers under state tort laws, avoiding federal courts. Tort laws prohibit assault, battery, infliction of emotional distress, and invasion of privacy. This type of suit makes the harasser individually legally liable.

Courts have refused to permit some organizations to pay the legal costs, ordering the convicted individuals themselves to pay out of their own pockets.

"I need this to be faxed to the Stockholm office until you get a 'yes'."

Sexual Harassment vs. Sex Discrimination

Title VII of the Civil Rights Act of 1964 prohibits discrimination in employment. Many people confuse sexual harassment and sex discrimination. In fact, sexual harassment is only one kind of sex discrimination. Both are actions prohibited by state and federal law.

What actions would be considered discrimination on the basis of sex, but not sexual harassment? List three you believe fall into this category:

1. ______________________________

2. ______________________________

3. ______________________________

In cases of sexual harassment, sex is made a term or condition of employment. In discrimination on the basis of sex, a member or members of one sex are treated differently than those of the other sex.

Part Summary

- In 1980, the Equal Employment Opportunity Commission (EEOC) issued *Guidelines on Sexual Harassment in the Workplace*. Although guidelines are not law, the U.S. Supreme Court has said the EEOC Guidelines should be accorded the same weight as laws

- The EEOC Guidelines describe sexual harassment as: Unwelcome sexual advances, requests for sexual favors, and other verbal or physical conduct of a sexual nature, when:

  a) Submission to such conduct is made explicitly or implicitly a term or condition of an individual's employment.

  b) Submission to or rejection of such conduct by an individual is used as the basis for employment decisions affecting the individual.

  c) Such conduct has the purpose or effect of unreasonably interfering with an individual's work performance or creating an intimidating, hostile, or offensive working environment.

- Sexual harassment ranges from verbal actions, such as risqué jokes, to unwanted and inappropriate physical actions or attacks. Intentional or not, all sexual harassment is aggression against another person's body or psyche.

- *Vicarious liability* is the liability that a supervisory party, such as an employer, bears for the conduct of an associate or subordinate even if the organization did not know about the harassment.

- An *affirmative defense* must show that the employer exercised reasonable care to prevent and promptly corrected any harassing behavior and that the employee unreasonably failed to take advantage of any preventive or corrective opportunities provided by the employer.

- When an individual who has been sexually harassed seeks legal counsel, it is possible that the organization, as well as the individual who is accused of being the harasser, will have to pay damages.

- Sexual discrimination occurs when members of one sex are treated differently than those of the other sex.

P A R T **3**

Preventing Sexual Harassment in the Workplace

In this part:

- Developing a Policy Against Sexual Harassment
- Communicating the Organization's Policy
- Instituting Training to Prevent Harassment
- Counseling Employees Who Have Felt Harassed
- Handling Employee Privacy Concerns

Developing a Policy Against Sexual Harassment

Sexual harassment is very expensive. At the very least, it causes low morale and consequently decreases productivity. Angry, fearful, humiliated people are incapable of performing well. If not addressed, sexual harassment may result in expensive lawsuits, dreadful publicity, and the destruction of an organizational image that took years to build.

Although sexual harassment is illegal, its elimination will come through organizational and individual commitment, not the courts. Most individuals, men and women, want a safe and secure workplace, free from intimidation and fear.

Three Approaches

An organization can take an important step toward creating a safe, secure, positive work environment by implementing a strong sexual harassment policy. There are three approaches to take in policy development:

1. A broad anti-harassment/positive-environment policy that includes a statement specifically addressing sexual harassment
2. A separate sexual harassment policy that covers all organizational members
3. Separate sexual harassment policies—one that addresses non-management employees and one that addresses management

The following pages provide examples of each of these approaches.

Approach 1: A Broad Anti-harassment Statement

To: All Employees

Subject: Working Atmosphere Statement

Policy Against Harassment of Employees

All employees have a responsibility to maintain high standards of honesty and integrity and to conduct themselves in a manner that will ensure proper performance of the organization's business.

Working Atmosphere

It is the policy of this organization to provide a working atmosphere free from discriminatory insult, intimidation, and other forms of harassment. All employees share the responsibility for fostering a pleasant working atmosphere that allows individuals to achieve high performance in their duties. Harassment is also prohibited by state and federal anti-discrimination laws.

Harassment

Harassment based on race, religion, color, national origin, age, sex, or sexual orientation is a violation of the organization's policy. Harassment may be overt or subtle, but whatever form it takes—verbal, nonverbal, or physical—harassment is insulting and demeaning to the recipient and cannot be tolerated in the workplace. Examples of harassment are verbal abuse; racial, ethnic, and religious epithets; slurs or jokes; graffiti (remarks written or drawn on walls or other structures); obscene gestures; and hazing. Even derogatory remarks between friends may lead to overt acts of discrimination.

Sexual Harassment

Sexual harassment is intolerable in the workplace. It includes unwelcome sexual advances, requests for sexual favors, and other verbal or physical conduct of a sexual nature when such conduct is made explicitly or implicitly a term or condition of employment, is used as a basis for employment decisions, or has the purpose or effect of interfering with work performance or creating an otherwise offensive working environment.

Employee Responsibility

Employees who believe that they or another employee are being harassed by someone on the premises should promptly report the harassing conduct to management. Incidents may be reported to the immediate supervisor, EEO coordinator, Human Resources manager, or plant management.

Management Responsibility

All members of management are responsible for ensuring that no harassment occurs within their area of authority. Harassment complaints should receive immediate attention and be reported to the EEO coordinator. Investigations will be conducted in cooperation with the EEO coordinator and may include conferring with parties and witnesses named by the complaining employee. Because of the sensitive nature of such complaints, incidents must be investigated with particular care and should remain, to the extent possible, strictly confidential.

Sanctions

If the investigation reveals that the complaint is valid, then prompt action, sufficient to stop the harassment immediately and to prevent its recurrence, will be taken. This may include disciplinary action up to and including discharge. Should the investigation reveal that an employee has become the victim of harassment by a non-employee, it will be the responsibility of the EEO coordinator to take the appropriate action in dealing with the vendor, contractor, or other employer of the person involved.

Designated Counselors

(List the names of the designated counselors.)

____

____

____

____

Approach 2: Specific Policy on Sexual Harassment

It is the policy of this organization for all employees to be able to work in an environment free from all forms of discrimination, including sexual harassment. Sexual harassment refers to behavior that is unwelcome and personally offensive, and that hurts morale and interferes with work effectiveness.

The EEOC has adopted written guidelines stating that any sexual harassment tolerated by employers constitutes a violation of Title VII of the Civil Rights Act of 1964.

EEOC Guidelines

Unwelcome sexual advances, requests for sexual favors, and other verbal or physical conduct of a sexual nature constitute sexual harassment when (1) submission to such conduct is made either explicitly or implicitly a term or condition of an individual's employment, (2) submission to or rejection of such conduct by an individual is used as the basis for employment decisions affecting such individual, or (3) such conduct has the purpose or effect of substantially interfering with an individual's work performance or creating an intimidating, hostile, or offensive working environment.

Violation of this rule will be the basis for appropriate discipline, up to and including termination.

It is the responsibility of each member of management to provide the necessary support to ensure that discrimination in employment does not occur and that associates are assured of a workplace free from sexual harassment. All members of management should be advised of this policy and are accountable for its effective administration throughout their respective organizations.

All associates are encouraged to promptly bring violations of this policy to the attention of Human Resources or their management. Should a manager or supervisor be advised of an infraction of this policy, the incident should be reported immediately to [*Human Relations or the manager of Employee Relations*].

Approach 3: Separate Policies for Employees and Supervisors

Sample Policy for All Employees

It is the Company's policy to prohibit harassment of one employee by another employee or supervisor on the basis of sex. Although it is not easy to define precisely what harassment is, it certainly includes unwelcome sexual advances, requests for sexual favors, and other verbal or physical conduct of a sexual nature, such as uninvited touching or sexually related comments. Any employee who feels sexually harassed should immediately report the matter to ____________________.

Violations of this policy will not be tolerated and may result in discipline, up to and including discharge.

Sample Policy for Supervisors

It is the Company's policy to prohibit harassment of one employee by another on the basis of sex. Although it is not easy to define precisely what harassment is, it certainly includes unwelcome sexual advances, requests for sexual favors, and other verbal or physical conduct of a sexual nature, such as uninvited touching or sexually related comments.

All members of management should be advised of this policy and held accountable for the effective administration of its intent throughout their respective organizations. Should a manager or supervisor be advised of an infraction of this policy, the incident should be reported immediately to ______________________.

Violations of this policy will not be tolerated and may result in discipline, up to and including discharge.

WHAT IS YOUR ORGANIZATION'S POLICY?

Answer the following questions to find out how much you know about your organization's sexual harassment policy.

1. Where can you find a copy of your organization's sexual harassment policy?

   ____

2. The policy is prominently displayed in the following locations:

   ____

   ____

3. ____________ times a year, I discuss organizational personnel policies, including sexual harassment, with those who report to me.

4. If an employee in my organization wants to report having been sexually harassed, the procedure the person would follow is:

   ____

   ____

5. My personal responsibilities regarding sexual harassment are:

   ____

   ____

How well did you do? Your answers to this exercise will give you an idea of how well your organization has implemented its sexual harassment policy. The following three steps are required for effective implementation and for complying with state and federal laws:

1. Communication
2. Training
3. Counseling

The next sections look at each of these steps in more detail.

Communicating the Organization's Policy

The best policy against sexual harassment is useless if it is not communicated effectively. Even if the organization already has a well-written policy, it is important to publicize it regularly. The best strategy is to use all of the following methods at various times throughout the year.

Permanent Posting

The customary and most logical place to post the policy is on the same bulletin boards as EEO, Occupational Safety and Health Administration, and other policy information.

Memos

When implementing a new sexual harassment policy, disseminate it throughout the organization, accompanied by an appropriate memo emphasizing its importance and stating that the organization will not tolerate harassment. If a policy is already in place, distribute a reminder memo at least once a year.

Articles

Several approaches can be taken with newsletter articles. Sexual harassment policy can be publicized:

- In a general article discussing positive work environments, positive interpersonal relations at work, fairness, and gender and cultural differences
- In an article specifically addressing sexual harassment and its negative effects on both individuals and the organization, reiterating the organization's policy and procedures to address complaints
- As part of an EEO article discussing affirmative action and discrimination, including sexual harassment

Sexual harassment, equal employment, and affirmative action are sensitive topics. People often see sexual harassment as an issue only for overly sensitive females. An effective article is one that establishes a tone that informs rather than alienates. Such an article can be a useful tool against harassment when it contains data and facts that demonstrate the extent of harassment and its negative effects and costs—monetary and otherwise—for the victim, the harasser, and the organization.

Meetings

For new employees, both non-management and management, orientation should cover the organization's human resources policies and procedures, including the sexual harassment policy. Managers should review and discuss the organization's policies and procedures routinely in their department meetings. This makes it easy to address sexual harassment without overemphasizing it.

No employee at any level should be able to claim ignorance of a policy as an excuse for an inappropriate behavior.

Training

Education is essential for preventing sexual harassment and for effectively handling complaints when they occur.

Do You "Know It When You See It"?

Before starting this exercise, review the *EEOC Guidelines on Sexual Harassment*. Then check (✓) the situations below that you think would be considered sexual harassment.

___ 1. Person A repeatedly requests a date, even though Person B declines every invitation and makes it clear he or she is not interested.

___ 2. A male supervisor looks women up and down while he is having a conversation with them.

___ 3. A female worker wears tight miniskirts to work, which provoke some of her male co-workers to make sexual comments and jokes about her.

___ 4. A male employee hangs a calendar with nude pictures on the wall of his private office. A female co-worker is offended when she goes into his office to pick up a report from his desk.

___ 5. A female supervisor asks a male subordinate to work late and have dinner with her. At dinner, she makes repeated comments with sexual overtones, making him uncomfortable.

___ 6. A supervisor and staff of three men and two women have lunch to celebrate a staff member's birthday. One of the men tells a joke with sexual overtones. Everyone laughs except one of the women, who is offended. When she says so, everyone tells her she is too sensitive and is ruining their fun.

___ 7. A male vice president's female assistant declines an invitation by a major male client to go out for coffee. The client repeats the request and she declines again. The client complains to the vice president that the assistant is too sensitive, unfriendly, and not good for business.

___ 8. A female manager has an opening in her department. Three qualified individuals apply, including a male whom she used to date. She hires a woman she believes will be the best with clients. The man complains to the manager's boss that his not being hired is sexual harassment because of their past relationship.

Some of these situations are complex. The following exercise will help you explore the issues raised.

Compare your answers with the authors' analysis in the Appendix.

EXPLORING YOUR OWN BELIEFS

How do you react to the situations described in the preceding exercise? The questions below will help you explore your own thoughts and feelings on these issues.

Is a woman responsible for harassment when she flirts or wears suggestive clothing? What if that woman is raped? Is she responsible then?

____

____

____

When is clothing or behavior suggestive, and by whose definition?

____

____

____

How do you feel about flirting by men or women at work?

____

____

____

How do you feel about jokes and remarks with sexual overtones in the workplace?

____

____

____

CONTINUED

CONTINUED

How would you see these situations if the gender of the persons were reversed?

____

____

____

How would you see these situations if they were the same, but the individuals were of the same sex?

____

____

____

If an office with both men and women works well with a lot of joking and occasional sexual banter, but one person finds it offensive, how do you feel about this situation? Will strict enforcement of a sexual harassment policy suppress all fun at work?

____

____

____

Instituting Training to Prevent Harassment

This book is likely to make you increasingly aware of the complexities and subtleties of confronting and preventing harassment. Because of this complexity and the differences in what individuals consider sexual harassment, training is crucial for prevention and for dealing effectively with sexual harassment complaints when they occur.

Some states have enacted laws mandating at least two hours of sexual harassment prevention education for all supervisory employees. These laws also require that employers provide at least two hours of follow-up training and education for all supervisory employees every two years for as long as these employees have supervisory authority.

Four Steps to Effective Training

The steps in designing and implementing a comprehensive training program are:

1. Conduct a sexual harassment audit or attitude survey.
2. Design the training.
3. Implement the training.
4. Evaluate the program.

For broad organizational problem solving and ownership of outcomes, your organization may want to create a task force, which would include individuals from various backgrounds and organizational levels. This task force could be designated to address sexual harassment only, or broader interpersonal concerns and issues.

Step 1: Auditing Current Policies and Patterns

It is not recommended that an organization rush out suddenly, with no warning, and ask every individual about sexual harassment. But there are effective and efficient ways to find out how pervasive harassment is and where it may be occurring. These same strategies can be used to discover other discriminatory and inappropriate interpersonal behavior throughout the organization.

Review of Policies, Procedures, and Management Styles

The audit should begin with a review of all Human Resources policies, procedures, and practices, including management styles. To be effective, this review must answer the following questions:

- Are policies and procedures clearly stated? Will they enable everyone in the organization to know exactly what is acceptable and unacceptable behavior? Is it clear what one must do to address a problem or issue a complaint?
- Does management live the policies and procedures, or merely give them lip service? How do you know?
- Do individuals believe that they can address problems and file complaints without repercussion? How do you know?
- When an investigation occurs, how is privacy honored?
- Are investigations handled consistently and fairly, regardless of the organizational level of the individuals involved? How do you know this?

Review of Terminations

An organization may have a few honest people who, in a termination interview, will tell you they are leaving because of harassment. But do not count on it. For a more accurate search:

- Analyze termination data. Is turnover higher in certain areas or departments or under a particular manager? Why?
- Review unemployment compensation filings. Sexual harassment may surface as a reason.

If terminations are higher in certain areas, an investigation may be appropriate. Patterns usually exist, particularly when a supervisor or manager is the harasser.

Review of Organizational Structure

Sexual harassment is harder to detect in autocratic, pyramidal organizational structures than it is in matrix organizations. This is true whether the harasser is the supervisor or another employee.

Harassment can remain hidden within a department because communication is primarily vertical and formal rather than across departments. The extensive coordination and relating among departments that occurs in matrix organizations makes hiding any problem or issue difficult.

Review of Human Resources

The manner in which the Human Resources department works can have a dramatic effect on organizational attitudes toward equality, sexual harassment, and relationships among organization members. Several areas deserve special scrutiny:

- Recruitment and selection policies and practices
- The performance evaluation and management system
- Training

When you're reviewing recruitment and selection policies, procedures, and practices, ask:

- Are these policies and practices unbiased and non-discriminatory?
- Is selection based on more than one person's decision and on well-defined criteria?

The organization may want to pay special attention to practices in remote locations and field operations, where inappropriate practices and behavior can easily occur undetected.

Human Resources should review all individual evaluations with below-satisfactory ratings to verify that such a rating is deserved. The following questions will assist in making such a determination:

- What was the individual's previous performance?
- Have there been previous performance problems in the same department or area? If so, is there any pattern?
- Does the supervisor have sufficient and appropriate documentation?
- What type of improvement plan has been initiated and was it mutually agreed upon?

Effective and routine monitoring of appraisals can be an excellent tool for the early detection of problems.

Reinforcement of Negative Behaviors

It has long been known, both in psychological circles and in performance management practice, that people continue or eliminate behaviors depending on the reinforcement they receive.

To identify whether negative behaviors are being reinforced in the organization, the sexual harassment audit should include these questions:

- What kinds of attitudes and behavior patterns are reinforced?
- In meetings where the attendees are predominantly male, what kinds of jokes and remarks are made that might make a woman feel unwanted or harassed?
- How do women treat men in a predominantly female department?
- How do people in your organization talk about gays and lesbians?
- How do men talk about women in the organization when they are not present? And vice versa?

The final question is especially important because an organization's real culture and environment are generally established informally behind closed doors. The environment includes setting examples. Individuals in lower ranks tend to model the behavior of higher-ranking, successful people. What behaviors do the executives in your organization model?

When claims of sexual harassment are raised, the manner in which everyone involved is treated can either encourage harassment or deter it. And how the complaint is handled may either encourage or discourage others when they're deciding whether to come forward in the future. If those who complain have been branded as troublemakers in the past, harassment might be occurring and the organization might not even be aware of it because people are afraid to complain.

What You Can Do

Depending on your position in the organization, you might not be able to answer all of the questions or address the issues in this audit. Nevertheless, you can be a model for others, and you can share this book with those who do affect policies, procedures, and practices in the organization. No one is powerless. Each individual in an organization affects the total culture and environment.

IS YOUR ORGANIZATION REINFORCING HARASSMENT?

Here is a worksheet for recording your answers to the questions presented in the preceding section. These answers will help you identify whether your organization is inadvertently reinforcing behaviors that qualify as sexual harassment.

What kinds of attitudes and behavior patterns are reinforced?

____

____

In meetings where the attendees are predominantly male, what kinds of jokes and remarks are made that might make a woman feel unwanted or harassed?

____

____

How do women treat men in a predominantly female department?

____

____

How do people in your organization talk about gays and lesbians?

____

____

How do men talk about women in the organization when they are not present? And vice versa?

____

____

AUDIT YOUR OWN BEHAVIOR

This exercise will help you uncover any discriminatory or inappropriate interpersonal behaviors of your own.

How do you relate to others in your department and in the organization? Do you treat people differently depending on their sex or sexual orientation?

What jokes or comments have you made that someone might consider sexual harassment?

How do you know whether people did or did not feel harassed?

When someone makes a joke or comment that you consider inappropriate or harassing, you…

AUDIT YOUR AREA OR DEPARTMENT

If you supervise others, go back and review your answers to the "Audit Your Own Behavior" exercise. Then go over the organizational audit questions in this worksheet and apply the questions to your area or department only.

How do people under your supervision know about organizational policies and procedures?

____

____

When was the last time someone in your department complained about a concern or issue? How did you handle it?

____

____

____

How do you know that you handle situations honestly and consistently?

____

____

What is the turnover rate in your area?

____

____

Why did people leave?

____

____

____

CONTINUED

CONTINUED

When you hire a new person, what criteria do you use for selection?

____

____

When you last hired a new person, would it have made a difference if the person were of a different sex?

____

____

How do you know?

____

____

If someone from outside your area interviewed your employees about your management practices, how would those you supervise describe you?

____

____

____

Now review your responses to the reinforcement exercise. How would you change your answers if they applied only to you and your department?

____

____

____

____

Step 2: Designing the Training Program

The goal of the training program is to give individuals the support, guidance, and reinforcement needed to develop and consistently use effective interpersonal skills with all people, regardless of sex, ethnic origin, and other differences.

There are several ways an organization might go about training employees on sexual harassment. The training could be:

- A specific program based on needs as determined from the audit
- Part of a general management skills program that includes a segment on sexual harassment
- A separate sexual harassment program
- A combination of the above options

Course Material

The organization must decide whether to use prepackaged material or develop its own. One effective option is to use ready-made audio-visual material as part of an overall program designed to meet specific organizational needs.

Effective training is conducted initially in the classroom and includes continuous on-the-job feedback and development. At a minimum, effective classroom training on sexual harassment must:

- Cover basic information on federal and state laws and major court cases
- Provide examples of effective and appropriate behavior for handling various situations
- Include reviewing and discussing complex case studies and examples
- Provide the opportunity to practice appropriate interpersonal skills in challenging situations

CASE STUDY: Harassment in the Warehouse?

Alex Jordan worked for the XYZ Corporation for many years. When he started working in the warehouse, the company made boxes and other containers.

For the last five years, Alex has managed three warehouses and a large distribution network. He has a large staff, mostly of clerks, inventory people, warehouse workers, and drivers. Until the last few years, almost everyone working for him was male. Now he has two female clerks, one female driver, and two women working in one of the warehouses. On the whole, he thinks the men reacted well to having women around. At first, there was some teasing and joking, but it did not last long. He thought everything was going smoothly, until about six months ago.

James Roachman is a new driver. He has an excellent record from his previous jobs. He is tall, strong, and clean-cut—just the sort of guy Alex feels comfortable with. Two months ago, one of the other drivers, Josh Strong, overheard James on the telephone. From James's words and tone, Josh surmised that this was a conversation between romantic partners. Josh went to Alex very upset, because he was sure that the other individual on the telephone was a male. Alex told Josh it was none of his business and to go back to work.

It has not turned out to be that simple. Alex overheard Josh make negative comments about gays within James's hearing. At first, James did nothing and Alex ignored it, hoping it would all go away. Instead, the negative comments increased. Josh started talking about James to others. Some of the other workers began avoiding James.

Two days ago, James came to Alex complaining that someone had left a threatening note on the seat of his truck. He threatened to go to the Civil Rights Commission to complain of sexual harassment. Alex promised to do something. But two days have passed and he has done nothing. He feels extremely uncomfortable with the situation and does not know what to say or do about it.

CONTINUED

CONTINUED

Is This Sexual Harassment?

The following questions will help you explore your beliefs in relation to this case. Write your responses on the lines provided.

1. Is this case an example of sexual harassment? Why or why not?

____

____

____

2. What should Alex do?

____

____

____

3. If James goes to the EEOC or a state agency, what will be the general procedure?

____

____

____

4. Which of your organization's policies and procedures would apply in a situation like this?

____

____

____

Compare your answers with the authors' responses in the Appendix.

Step 3: Implementing the Training

Ideally, any training program that includes sexual harassment should be mandatory for every person working for the company. Otherwise, those who need the training most will not attend.

Take It from the Top

Nothing sets a more negative tone than for lower-level employees to discover that senior executives and management have not gone through training. Of course such training will not be identical for individuals at all levels. But all staff—executives, management, and non-management—should be trained to spot and handle instances of discrimination.

Executives need only look throughout the lower ranks of their organization to see and hear their own behaviors. The greatest impact on the behavior of everyone in the organization comes from the way the executives behave. They set the tone, and others follow.

What is the official executive position on sexual harassment in your organization?

____

____

What is the informal attitude in your organization toward sexual harassment? How does this differ from the formal policy, if at all?

____

____

Have you ever seen or heard an executive in your organization engage in behavior that might be interpreted as harassment? What happened?

____

____

To merge the organization's formal policies and informal practices, the key executives must go through the training and make it known that they and the organization will not tolerate harassing behavior.

Timing the Training

Communication of the organization's formal policies can be part of the introductory training or orientation material or be sent separately to all organizational members in a memo introducing the training. The task force can help decide method which would be more appropriate and effective.

Generally, it takes at least a half day to cover laws, policies, and procedures and to give examples of effective behavior. Another half day can be devoted to case studies and discussions, with practice in handling difficult situations. Managers also need training on how to handle complaints, both procedurally and emotionally.

Self-Check for Managers

As a manager, are you modeling positive behavior for others to follow? To explore this issue, write your answers to the questions below.

Describe how the men and women who work for you interrelate.

____

____

How do you feel about the way the men and women in your area work together?

____

____

Which of their behaviors, if any, could be interpreted as sexual harassment? In what way(s)?

____

____

What have you done about it?

____

____

How would you feel and what would you do if sexual harassment happened to you?

____

____

What kind of tone regarding sexual harassment do you set for your department?

____

____

Step 4: Evaluating the Training's Effectiveness

The organization has set policies and procedures, completed an audit, and implemented training. How will you know if it is working?

The effectiveness of any system depends on continued feedback and readjustment. After training has taken place, revisit the initial audit questions. Have situations improved? Have new problems arisen? What adjustments in policies, procedures, and practices need to be made?

The never-ending process of evaluation is crucial for effectiveness.

The benefits are many for organizations that demonstrate a culture of respect and civility for all employees and that value individuals for their contributions. Such organizations reap the rewards of greater productivity, fewer complaints, and general employee satisfaction and loyalty.

"Sandy, how could you accuse me of sexual harassment?"

Counseling Employees Who Have Felt Harassed

The legitimacy of an organization's sexual harassment policies and procedures depends greatly on how the organization deals with individuals who feel they have been harassed. The emotional aftereffects of any kind of harassment and abuse are strong and include feelings of loss and grief, anger and depression. Guilt and self-blame are particularly detrimental to the recovery process.

CASE STUDY: Salma and the VP

Salma Smith, a 40-year-old analyst in your department, comes into your office, looking nervous and upset. She seems to be on the verge of tears. You ask her to sit down and you inquire about the problem. With difficulty, she tells you that she feels she has been sexually harassed by the vice president of this division.

She claims he asked her out several times and she always made excuses for why she could not go. Lately, he has come into her office, brushed against her, and made remarks about her lack of cooperation.

She says she did not come to you before because she was embarrassed and afraid; after all, he is a vice president. She asks you what she should do. She says she cannot take his attitude and actions any longer and has thought about quitting, but needs the job. She is a single parent.

Describe how you would handle this situation.

____

____

____

If Salma were Sam, a male, what would be your reaction?

____

____

____

Compare your answers with the authors' responses in the Appendix.

Recommended Course of Action

Rarely will a manager or Human Resources professional possess the expertise to provide in-depth counseling. Even if the individual appears to be emotionally sound, it is advisable to suggest referral sources. If the organization has an employee assistance program, suggest that the person may want to talk with someone there.

When an individual comes to you with a complaint of sexual harassment:

- Be supportive and empathetic.
- Carefully explain the procedures that will be followed.
- Emphasize that the complaint is serious and will be handled as such.
- Explain that separate counseling is available and explain where to find it.

Letting the individual know that the situation will be thoroughly investigated, privately and discreetly, is important psychologically as well as legally. Victims are often afraid to speak out because they think their jobs may be in jeopardy and because they fear an invasion of privacy.

If you are not the appropriate person to investigate the complaint, explain the procedure. Offer to initiate the process.

Cultural Considerations

Individuals from different cultures may react differently to sexual harassment. Some may not be inclined to pursue the matter. Some may not understand the law and their rights. Some may not speak the language. Organizations need to be sensitive to the difficulties their employees face in coming forward with a complaint and having that complaint resolved.

Handling Employee Privacy Concerns

As with any sensitive interpersonal matter, sexual harassment complaints must be handled with utmost privacy. If they are not, individuals will be exceedingly reluctant to come forward and discuss the situation with anyone in the organization. Handling complaints internally is far preferable to the individual's seeking outside help first.

Your organization should have a procedure for handling all complaints, not just those involving sexual harassment. This procedure should guarantee maximum privacy for the complaining party, while allowing for necessary investigative activities.

In a union environment, this process might be called a grievance procedure. Regardless of its label, the procedure should:

- Be clear and easy to understand
- Be described step by step so that everyone knows exactly what will happen and when
- Emphasize that all problems and investigations will be handled discreetly

Generally speaking, individuals should address complaints initially to their immediate supervisor, unless that person is the problem. This option should be well publicized to encourage employees to raise the issue if it exists. With sexual harassment, it is also advisable to involve Human Resources or Employee Relations immediately.

CASE STUDY: Heather Requests Privacy

Heather Thomas, a young employee, new to the organization, comes to your office. You supervise an area that works with her department. She tells you that another employee in her area has been harassing her, leaving suggestive notes and cartoons on her desk. She tells you she can handle the situation and does not want you to tell her supervisor or to involve Human Resources.

1. Should you respect Heather's request for privacy and do nothing?

____

____

____

2. What problems do you create for the organization if you do nothing, as she requested?

____

____

____

3. Do you think the situation is more dangerous if you are a Human Resources manager?

____

____

____

Compare your answers with the authors' responses in the Appendix.

Part Summary

- When you're developing a sexual harassment policy, there are three approaches to take:
  - A broad anti-harassment/positive-environment statement
  - A separate sexual harassment policy that covers all organizational members
  - Separate sexual harassment policies for management and non-management personnel
- To communicate your sexual harassment policies, you can permanently post it, send memos, write newsletter articles, hold meetings, and provide training.
- The four steps in effective training are:
  1. Conduct a sexual harassment audit or attitude survey.
  2. Design the training.
  3. Implement the training.
  4. Evaluate the program.
- When an individual comes to you with a complaint of sexual harassment:
  - Be supportive and empathetic.
  - Carefully explain the procedures that will be followed.
  - Emphasize that the complaint is serious and will be handled as such.
  - Explain that separate counseling is available and described where to find it.
- Your organization should have a procedure that guarantees maximum privacy for the complaining party while allowing for necessary investigative activities.

PART 4

Handling Sexual Harassment Complaints

In this part:

- Investigating Sexual Harassment
- Choosing Suitable Investigators
- Collecting Documentation
- Interviewing the Complainant
- Interviewing the Accused
- Interviewing the Witnesses
- Resolving the Complaint

Investigating Sexual Harassment

To determine if sexual harassment has occurred in a given situation, the courts and the agencies investigating complaints of sexual harassment look at what the EEOC calls the *totality of the circumstances*. The process includes identifying the steps the organization has taken to address the problem.

Since several important Supreme Court decisions in the late 1990s, the courts ask not only if the organization has a policy prohibiting sexual harassment, but also about how conscientiously that policy is publicized and followed. The policy your organization uses should be posted or appear in the employee handbook, should be permanently displayed on your organization's bulletin boards, and should appear in the organization's policy manual.

Your organization's legal department or an outside attorney should review the policy to ensure that it does not create unknown or unintended obligations for the organization.

In-house Investigation

In investigating the complaint, the investigator should:

- Make certain to understand the complaint
- Interview the complainant and get all facts before doing other investigations
- Interview all possible witnesses—co-workers, supervisors, customers
- Interview the accused
- Gather all relevant documentation
- Make a report on the investigation
- If appropriate, make a recommendation for action

Maintaining Confidentiality

All investigations of claims of discrimination should be handled promptly and be kept confidential. In part, this is required because anti-discrimination laws prohibit retaliating against a claimant who exercises his or her right to raise the claim. Potential libel or slander actions by the accused are other factors to be considered.

Although the investigation should be handled confidentially, some matters cannot always be kept confidential. Consider the following situation.

You receive a complaint of sexual harassment by an employee who claims that some of her male co-workers have made offensive jokes with sexual innuendoes in her presence. She has asked them to stop. She claims that one of the co-workers even brought an X-rated video to the office. He told her to take it home, watch it, and think of him. She is afraid that if her co-workers know she has complained, they will make working in the area even more difficult. She is not the only female in the area.

You may be able to conduct the necessary interviews without revealing the name of the complainant. Questions can be phrased in terms of what goes on in the workplace on an ongoing basis, rather than "Did you tell a dirty joke while Jane was in the office?"

Here are some questions you might ask about the workplace in general:

- "Do you joke around?"
- "Does everyone participate in the banter?"
- "What kind of jokes are told?"
- "Does everyone tell jokes?"
- "Does the supervisor participate, too?"
- "Has anyone ever asked that the jokes stop?"

Choosing Suitable Investigators

In addition to having a policy against sexual harassment, an organization must take steps to demonstrate to its employees that the policy is important. The first step is choosing one or two people to accept and investigate complaints of sexual harassment.

Would it matter if the person(s) you chose were male or female? Would women be more likely to take their complaints to other women? Should the person appointed be one of the supervisors or an owner of the organization? Should the person appointed have been a victim of sexual harassment? Should the person considered for the job have any specialized training?

What attributes would you look for in choosing an investigator? List them below:

____

____

____

Now compare your responses to the authors' recommendations below.

Recommended Attributes

Individuals conducting the investigation need to be knowledgeable about the organization and its employees. They need to be familiar with good investigative techniques, including interviewing people and reviewing documentation. Sometimes it may be important to use the organization's legal counsel or outside counsel.

The sex of the investigator is not relevant. Some organizations have both a male and a female investigator. Those chosen to investigate should be viewed by employees as individuals with integrity. They should also be well respected at all levels of the organization.

Duties of Investigators

1. Make certain they understand the complaint.
2. Interview complainant and get all facts before doing any other investigations.
3. Interview all possible witnesses—co-workers, supervisors, and customers.
4. Interview the accused.
5. Gather all relevant documentation.
6. Make a report on the investigation.
7. If appropriate, make recommendations for action.

Collecting Documentation

Because of the complexity of the issues involved in claims of sexual harassment, supervisors and managers must use good documentation techniques in investigating claims.

Documentation should include:

- Interviews with witnesses, dated and signed by the investigator. Statements should be signed and dated by the witnesses.
- Relevant documents concerning the victim. These include:
  - Employment application
  - Reference checks
  - Evaluations for the entire employment period with the organization
  - Disciplinary warnings for all persons involved
  - Other memos concerning wage matters and promotions
- Documentation of any similar cases.
- Copies of any notes, cartoons, written threats, and so on.

NOTE: These are generic categories of documentation. Depending on the facts of a specific case, other documentation might need to be collected during the in-house investigation. Are there items that come to mind for a case you are dealing with or have dealt with? If so, list them on the following lines.

____

____

____

____

If the organization works regularly with a law firm, you may want to have that firm conduct the investigation to ensure confidentiality.

Interviewing the Complainant

When an employee complains of sexual harassment, the wise employer takes the complaint seriously. If you do not, a union organizer or the complainant's attorney might. The investigation may ultimately reveal that sexual harassment did not occur, but an investigation that includes an interview with the complainant should be initiated. This interview must be handled carefully.

Conducting the Interview

The complainant should be interviewed by one company representative. Although it might help to have two company representatives present at the interview, this might further intimidate the employee, who may already be the victim of some kind of intimidation.

If you are not a good note-taker, tape the interview. Inform the person that the interview will be taped and explain that you will use the tape recorder to ensure accuracy.

The interview should cover the following topics:

1. When did the sexual harassment occur? How long ago?
2. Over how long a period of time did the sexual harassment take place?
3. Did the sexual harassment happen at the office, the plant, a restaurant, or the complainant's or harasser's home?
4. Did the complainant ever tell the accused to stop, or reject the advances in any way? If not, why not?
5. If several weeks or months have passed since the sexual harassment occurred, find out why the complainant waited this long to report the harassment.
6. Identify names of witnesses, what they witnessed, and whether the complainant has discussed the claim with the witnesses.
7. Gather any other corroborating documentation of harassment.
8. Does the complainant have notes, letters, or other documentation claimed to have been written by the accused? If the complainant does have such documentation, ask to see it and make copies.

Are there other questions you think would be appropriate? If so, list them on the following lines.

____

____

Interviewing the Accused

Because the organization cares about its employees, as well as about potentially expensive lawsuits, the interview of the accused harasser also must be handled carefully.

Sometimes the accused may agree to be interviewed only if an attorney of his or her choosing is present. This is difficult because some attorneys may be disruptive while others may be helpful. Some organizations permit the attorney; others do not, taking the position that it is only an in-house investigation.

Although many women and men have been victims of sexual harassment, occasionally an employee will use a sexual harassment complaint to mask the real reason for being terminated, demoted, or passed over for a new job.

You must remember the concept of "not guilty unless proven otherwise." You do not want to be faced with a libel or slander lawsuit by the accused.

Other Considerations

Are there other things you want to keep in mind when interviewing the accused, in addition to the precautions necessary when interviewing the complainant? If so, list those below.

____

____

____

____

____

Interviewing Witnesses

Unless other persons claim to have been harassed by the accused, the organization may find it difficult, if not impossible, to determine if sexual harassment occurred.

In the majority of sexual harassment cases, the only people present, and therefore witnesses of the actions, are the victim and the accused. Although other persons may have been present in the work area, they might not have witnessed the alleged harassment.

Being Sensitive in Questioning

Despite a lack of witnesses, the organization must explore every area for facts and an understanding of what occurred. Persons in the work area should be interviewed. To protect the accused as well as the victim, consider how to conduct these interviews without revealing names.

To avoid potential slander actions by an accused person who is later found to be innocent, phrase questions as generally as possible. Begin with general background questions about the witness, such as length of employment, how long in the department, how long in the current job, prior experience, and likes and dislikes about the current job.

If the claim is that an employee was denied a promotion for rejecting the supervisor's advances, find out if others also applied for the job and what they believe about why someone else got the job.

If the claim is about a hostile work environment, then question possible witnesses generally, asking such questions as the following:

- "Have you seen anything unusual in the area?"
- "Do all employees in this area get along?"
- "Does everyone banter back and forth?"
- "Is there a lot of exchanging of jokes?"
- "Would you say the work area resembles a locker room?"

What other questions along these lines might you ask?

____

____

____

Resolving the Complaint

You have collected a lot of documentation and interviewed all witnesses. The steps you will take next are determined by what the investigation turned up. Do you think sexual harassment occurred, or was the investigation inconclusive?

When Sexual Harassment Has Occurred

You believe that sexual harassment has occurred. What steps will you take to resolve this situation? Depending on the circumstances, the resolution of the complaint should include some or all of the following actions:

- ▶ Consult with the complainant concerning an appropriate way to resolve the matter.
- ▶ If the employee was denied a promotion, consider placing the employee in the appropriate position.
- ▶ If the complainant lost wages, consider payment of those lost wages. If you do not, the complainant may obtain an agency or court order to be paid.
- ▶ An employee who transferred out of the job should be given the option of returning to that job.
- ▶ The accused should be terminated or issued a written warning.

If appropriate, prepare a settlement document, which should be reviewed by an attorney for the organization. The harassed employee should be permitted to have an attorney review the document.

When the Investigation Is Inconclusive

The guidelines just presented apply when your investigation substantiates charges of sexual harassment. What happens if the investigation is inconclusive?

You need to report the results of your investigation to the complainant as well as to the accused. The report to the complainant must:

- State that the investigation was inconclusive.
- Inquire whether the complainant can still work in that area of the organization. (If not, explore the possibility of a transfer to another area.)
- Counsel the complainant that if another incident occurs, it should be reported at once.

What else would you tell the employees involved? Speak with the employee who was accused. Emphasize that even though the investigation was inconclusive, any additional incidents will be investigated, and if they are substantiated, appropriate action, up to and including termination, will be taken.

Following the steps outlined in this section will remedy the problem, at least for the moment. If the employee subsequently retains a lawyer or seeks the assistance of an administrative agency, you will have placed your organization in a defensible position.

Review and Maintenance of Records

When the investigation is completed, place all documents in a separate file and keep them in a locked area in the personnel department.

Do *not* put them in the personnel file of the accused or of the person who is alleging the harassment. This caution is particularly important if the accused is later cleared of the charges.

CHECK YOUR ORGANIZATION'S PROGRESS

Courts today are taking a strong position on claims of sexual harassment. Because of this, all supervisors, managers, and employers must be educated about sexual harassment claims. Work through the following checklist to review your organization's progress toward this goal.

Check (✓) Yes or No to indicate which steps your company has taken to prevent sexual harassment in the workplace and to handle it effectively if it does happen.

	Yes	No
1. Does your organization offer regular training sessions to educate all employees about the implications of sexual harassment?	❑	❑
2. Has your organization appointed at least one representative to receive and investigate complaints of sexual harassment?	❑	❑
3. Is your organization representative a female?	❑	❑
4. Does your organization have two representatives, one male and one female, to receive and investigate complaints of sexual harassment?	❑	❑
5. Does your organization initiate investigations of complaints of sexual harassment immediately after the complaint is received?	❑	❑
6. Can an employee be terminated if he or she is found to have violated the organization's sexual harassment policy?	❑	❑
7. Does your organization maintain confidentiality when investigating complaints of sexual harassment?	❑	❑
8. Are victims of sexual harassment in your workplace involved in the decision on appropriate corrective actions to be taken?	❑	❑
9. If the complaint of sexual harassment is confirmed, are the terms and conditions of the victim's employment altered? (Is the victim moved to another work area while the harasser is left in place?)	❑	❑

CONTINUED

CONTINUED

Debrief

If your answer to question 5 is No, or you do not know, there is a problem. The courts have said that investigations should be initiated promptly.

If your answer to question 9 is Yes, do you know why this is done? Would you agree that this action victimizes the victim again? What alternatives might the organization implement?

____

____

____

The courts look at all the facts to determine whether sexual harassment occurred and to determine the appropriate damages. The steps the employer takes with regard to the accused and the victim are important aspects of that process.

"The ex-CEO left some big shoes to fill."

Part Summary

- The *totality of the circumstances* involves the process of identifying the steps the organization has taken to address a sexual harassment complaint. This process includes conducting an in-house investigation and maintaining confidentiality.
- The investigators need to understand the complaint, interview everyone involved to gather the facts, gather relevant documentation, write a report about the investigation, and make recommendations for action.
- When an employee complains of sexual harassment, the wise employer takes the complaint seriously and interviews the complainant, the accused, and any witnesses.
- If the investigation reveals that sexual harassment has occurred, the organization must take appropriate actions to resolve the matter. If the investigation is inconclusive, then both the complainant and the accused should be notified.

PART 5

Involving Governmental Agencies and the Courts

In this part:

- Seeking Assistance Outside the Organization
- Filing an Administrative Charge
- Settling the Case Through Mediation
- Understanding the Agency Investigative Process
- Receiving the Agency's Determination
- Going to Court

Seeking Assistance Outside the Organization

Although most employers today try to create an open atmosphere, employees often will not report sexual harassment to their supervisors or to Human Resources. The following are reasons given by persons who did not complain to their employer before seeking assistance outside the organization:

- Concern about retaliation from the supervisor, manager, or co-workers
- Lack of faith in the organization's investigative process
- A personal belief that because they were already terminated, nothing positive would result from their complaining to the organization
- Fear that other employees would learn about the complaint and gossip about it
- Concern that they might not find another job because they would be labeled troublemakers

As a result of these concerns, employees often will seek assistance from outsiders, including unions, attorneys, and federal and state administrative agencies charged with investigating discrimination claims. As noted earlier, within the United States, the EEOC is the federal agency that investigates sexual harassment charges.

Filing an Administrative Charge

Individuals who believe they have been sexually harassed can file a charge with the EEOC if the following requirements are met:

- The charge must be timely; that is, filed within 180 days of the alleged harassment or, if there is a state human rights agency, within 300 days of the alleged harassment.
- The complainant must be able to present what is called a *prima facie* (legally sufficient) case of sexual harassment.

It costs nothing to file a charge of discrimination. The charge process can be initiated through a letter. A phone call usually is not sufficient.

Even if the complainant cannot meet the above criteria, he or she can insist that charges be filed, and the agency must accept the charge. After the charge is filed, the law requires that it be served on the accused organization. This is usually done within 10 days. From the time the charge is filed, it can take as little as one week or as long as several years for it to be resolved. See the "Charge Process" chart, later in this section, for the steps that follow a charge of sexual harassment.

Local and State Agency Involvement

In many states, the charge process is handled by a state agency or local administrative agency that works with the EEOC in what is called a *sharing agreement*. Primarily because of heavy caseloads, such an agency normally will be the one to investigate the charge.

AGENCY AWARENESS

Although every state or local agency handles the investigation of a discrimination charge a little differently, the procedures the federal agency follows are the same throughout the United States. At least one office of the EEOC is in every state; some states have several offices.

What local or state agency in your area accepts and investigates complaints of discrimination?

____

Where in your area is it located?

____

Where is the EEOC office in your state?

____

The Charge Process

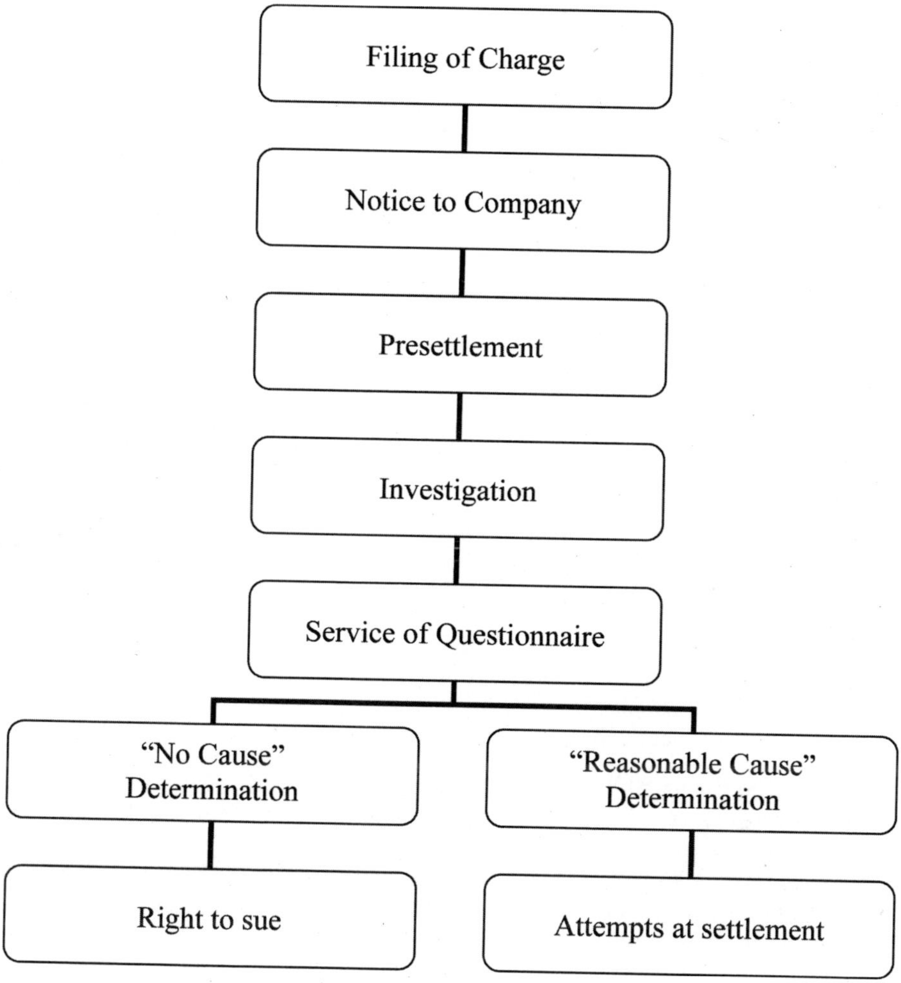

Settling the Case Through Mediation

In the late 1980s, the EEOC tested a settlement process called *mediation* in several of its offices across the country. Now this process is used in all EEOC offices.

After a charge of sexual harassment has been filed and before undertaking an investigation, the agency handling the charge will ask the employer whether the charge can be settled through mediation. A fast settlement may resolve the matter within weeks; an investigation can drag out over a year and the case still might not be resolved.

Why Settle Before an Investigation?

An employer might consider settling a charge of sexual harassment before it has been determined that it even occurred. The following are common reasons:

- To save costs associated with a lengthy investigation, including legal fees and the cost of taking managers away from their work
- To avoid an investigation by a state or federal agency which might uncover other problems
- For employee relations reasons, such as the impact of having outsiders on the work site
- A settle-all-problems attitude
- Knowledge that the harassment did occur

Employers who decide *not* to settle a sexual harassment charge at this stage may believe that settling cases early encourages other employees to file charges or lawsuits. Employers also may think that the settlement amount the employee seeks at this stage is not reasonable. In fact, however, sometimes cases that could have been settled for hundreds of dollars eventually result in thousands of dollars being spent on attorneys' fees and settlement later in the process.

The agencies know that employers will consider all of these factors when deciding if settlement is appropriate at this stage.

If an employer believes that sexual harassment has occurred, it should consider settling the case early in the charge process. The settlement may include a monetary award, development and publication of a sexual harassment policy if none exists, and discipline of the accused, including possible suspension, loss of wages, and termination of employment.

In settling a claim, the agency may want to use only its own settlement documents, which resolve the charge before the agency. An organization should consider employing a broad settlement document, ensuring that all possible claims of the employee, such as possible tort and contract claims, are resolved. A sample agreement is provided in the Appendix.

"You said if I wore makeup I'd be taken more seriously."

Understanding the Agency Investigative Process

A charge of sexual harassment is more difficult to investigate than other discrimination charges because most charges of sexual harassment come down to one person's word against another's. This section looks at what evidence, besides interviews of witnesses, will be necessary to resolve a charge of sexual harassment before an administrative agency.

Providing Information

After the agency sends a copy of the charge to the organization, it will forward a lengthy questionnaire. The information provided to an administrative agency on this questionnaire and in other ways may be *discoverable* if a case goes to court, which means that the information revealed may be released to the plaintiff in a lawsuit. It may also be seen by other federal or state agencies.

For these reasons, the response should be carefully considered and possibly limited to information that is specifically relevant to the sexual harassment charge. The organization's legal advisers should be involved in preparing the response to the administrative agency.

Documentation

For example, if the charge is that the employee was not promoted because of refusing to participate in a sexual relationship with the boss, documents relevant to this charge would include:

- Documents of other promotions or other types of personnel actions within the same department within the relevant time period—six months before or after the charge
- Documents of other persons who applied for promotions but were denied the job within a relevant time period—six months before the charge was filed
- A current EEO-1: a report completed by all employers with 100 or more employees, which shows how males, females, and minorities are employed within the organization
- A list of all persons recommended for promotion by the supervisor within the relevant time period
- Records of prior complaints by this employee or by other employees that involve this supervisor
- Disciplinary records concerning the complaining employee
- Disciplinary records concerning the alleged offender
- A copy of the organization's sexual harassment policy, as well as documentation of the steps the organization has taken to publicize it
- A copy of the training manual or other appropriate training materials used by the organization to sensitize all employees to the issue of sexual harassment
- A summary of the organization's investigation if it found no sexual harassment

Receiving the Agency's Determination

At the conclusion of its investigation, the EEOC normally issues a *Letter of Determination*. This summarizes the findings of the agency—that either there is *no reasonable or probable cause* to believe that sexual harassment has occurred, or there is *reasonable or probable cause* to believe that sexual harassment has occurred. If a state agency has conducted the investigation, it may issue its own determination.

Determination of No Cause

If the agency's investigation does not establish that discrimination occurred, then a required notice is issued. Some courts view this EEOC determination as closing the doors to further litigation on the issue. Whether this occurs depends on the way the investigative process was handled, the opportunity for both sides to cross-examine witnesses, and the evidence.

If the courts give the determination great weight, this outcome may be termed *collateral estoppel*, which prevents further litigation. Some courts may admit the determination into evidence, but give it little or no weight.

But this is not the end of the process. The agency will issue the complainant a letter known as a *right to sue*, which gives the complainant 90 days to file a lawsuit. At one time the courts were very liberal in appointing counsel to represent employees in discrimination cases. But courts have become much more restrictive in making such appointments. If the employee does not file his or her lawsuit within 90 days, the case is probably finished.

Determination of Reasonable or Probable Cause

If the EEOC finds cause to believe that sexual harassment occurred, it will attempt to conciliate or settle the case with the employer. If the case is not settled, the agency will decide whether to file a lawsuit against the employer in federal court.

If the complainant is represented by an attorney, the attorney will often request authority to file a lawsuit in court. Then the agency must give the complainant the right to sue. This may end the agency's involvement in the case.

If the case is closed before the agency at the request of the complainant's attorney, it is unlikely to be settled before suit is filed. For this reason, the organization should seriously consider settlement of the case at this stage.

Unlike a settlement at the start of the process, after a finding of discrimination, the agency will be looking for a remedy that makes the harassed individual *whole*, or puts the person where he or she would have been had the harassment not occurred. At this stage, the stakes and costs are much higher. If the case is not settled at this point, it will go to court. And the costs will quickly escalate.

Going to Court

Previously, a case brought under Title VII of the Civil Rights Act of 1964 could be tried only before a judge. But recent changes in the law may permit a trial before a jury. And claims involving personal injury (assault, battery, intentional infliction of emotional distress, invasion of privacy) can be tried before a jury.

Already an emotional and explosive issue, sexual harassment thus becomes extremely expensive because juries are made up of men and women who, if they have not been harassed themselves, may have friends or family who have been the victims of sexual harassment. Juries in such cases may award large judgments to plaintiffs.

A Multistep Process

Once a case involving claims of sexual harassment is filed, a lengthy and expensive process begins. Depending on how heavy the court docket is, the case may come to trial in six months or five years. In the interim, a process known as *discovery* will occur. Discovery is the learning of the claims, damages, and defenses of both sides. In this process, employees, managers, and supervisors are called on to answer questions, called *interrogatories*, and to testify under oath in depositions before a court reporter.

Anywhere in this process, settlement may occur. But if the complainant's attorney believes he or she has a strong case, settlement may be difficult or expensive.

Before the case is tried, a process called *summary judgment* may be undertaken. One side argues to the court, through a legal document, that there is no dispute about the facts and that based on current law, the case should be decided for either the employee or the organization before trial.

Courts do not readily grant motions for summary judgment. Because sexual harassment cases often involve conflicting testimony, courts hesitate to grant summary judgment. If summary judgment is denied, the case will be scheduled for trial.

Retaining Specialized Legal Counsel

You can see that if your organization is sued for sexual harassment in a state or federal court, you will want to be represented by an attorney who practices employment law. If your organization's attorney does not practice in this area, ask for a referral. Alternatively, your local bar association may have a lawyer referral panel.

Because labor law is so complex and ever changing, representation by counsel who has not previously handled such cases not only may be unnecessarily costly but also may result in your organization's losing its case. This is true during the investigative process as well as in court.

For example, in a recent Supreme Court case, a company that employed fewer than 15 employees was found to have violated the sections of the Civil Rights Act of 1964, as amended to deal with sexual harassment. The Court said that the company had waived the jurisdictional issue (that the EEOC can't investigate companies with fewer than 15 employees) by not objecting initially to the EEOC's investigation.

Part Summary

- Often, employees will seek assistance from outsiders, including attorneys and agency personnel, to investigate sexual harassment claims.
- Individuals who believe they have been sexually harassed can file a charge with the EEOC within 180 days of the alleged harassment, or within 300 days at a state human rights agency. Also, the complainant must be able to present a legally sufficient case of sexual harassment.
- The Charge Process has multiple steps: filing a charge, notifying the company, agreeing on a presettlement, investigating the charge, and gathering documentation to support the claim.
- *Mediation* is a settlement process that is used to prevent a drawn-out investigation and court case. However, some employers decide not to settle because they believe that doing so will encourage other employees to file charges or lawsuits, or because they believe the settlement amount to be unreasonable.
- After the investigation, the EEOC issues a *Letter of Determination* that summarizes the findings and states whether there is *reasonable cause* or *no cause* to believe that sexual harassment has occurred.
    - If the Letter of Determination declares that no cause has been found, the complainant has 90 days to file a lawsuit, or the case will mostly likely be closed.
    - If the Letter of Determination declares a reasonable or probable cause, the EEOC will attempt to settle the case with the employer. The stakes and costs are much higher after a finding of discrimination than they would be for a settlement at the start of the process. Once the case goes to court, the costs quickly escalate.
- Recent changes in the law permit a jury trial. Going to court is a lengthy process with many steps. The organization will need to retain specialized legal counsel.

PART 6

Maintaining a Positive Work Environment

In this part:

- Valuing a Harassment-Free Workplace
- Putting a Stop to Unwelcome Behavior

Valuing a Harassment-Free Workplace

Too often, organizations worry about sexual harassment only from the standpoint of legal costs and potential damages. This is a mistake. It is important also to consider the costs of lost time and productivity caused by an intimidating, hostile, or offensive working environment. Sexual harassment costs are pervasive.

Everyone wants a secure, safe place to work. Safety and security are what experts call *dissatisfiers*. If these elements are not present, people complain and productivity drops. Certainly safety and security are absent when sexual harassment occurs.

Elements of a Positive Work Environment

Safety and security alone, however, do not produce a positive environment or maximum productivity. To be productive, people have to:

- Feel safe and secure from overt physical and psychological harm
- Have good relationships with others with whom they work
- Feel respected for who they are and what they can contribute

Sexual harassment destroys all of these qualities. Implementing anti-harassment training has positive outcomes beyond preventing the harassment. It:

- Builds teamwork
- Teaches people how to constructively resolve conflicts at home as well as at work
- Helps people gain new understanding and respect for one another and their differences

All of these outcomes lead to improved productivity and organizational success.

For additional training ideas and material, read the Crisp Series book *Working Together: Succeeding in a Multicultural Organization* by George Simons.

CASE STUDY: Tom, the Killjoy?

Georgia Wise was head of the systems accounting area at a large international company. Most employees in her area had worked there for at least two years. It was a fun group with lots of teamwork. They were very busy, knew what needed to be accomplished, and were great at putting their heads together and getting things done.

It was also a relaxed atmosphere with a lot of bantering and joking, some of which was a bit sexual and contained a lot of innuendoes. It was fun, harmless teasing and no one seemed to care—that is, until Georgia hired Tom, a young man who, because of his specialized expertise, was able to solve problems the team had wrestled with for some time.

But Tom seemed very serious and uncomfortable with the rest of the group. The staff consistently asked him to come with them to lunch or breaks, but he always declined. Some employees complained that he did not belong and interfered with the overall team spirit.

Recently Georgia had been carefully watching the interactions in the department to try to figure out what was going on. She noticed Sandra approach Tom several times and make remarks about how good he looked, joking and teasing a bit. Tom did not look very happy about it. Another time, Amiel told a joke with sexual undertones. Tom was the only person who did not laugh.

What Would You Do?

Georgia did not want to endanger the fun teamwork that had been so effective in the past, but she had to do something about Tom. If you were Georgia, what would you do?

____

____

What could Tom do, assuming that he was uncomfortable about the sexual overtones of some of the jokes and banter?

____

____

Compare your answers with the authors' responses in the Appendix.

Putting a Stop to Unwelcome Behavior

People cannot read minds and frequently do not share beliefs and feelings. Much of the subtle behavior that might be tagged harassment continues to occur because the harasser has never been told that the behavior is affecting others. *Never assume* that someone else thinks as you do.

Anti-harassment training should emphasize these points, including a few fundamental do's and don'ts:

- DON'T touch another person in any way unless he or she has given you permission to do so. Do not make remarks that could be construed as harassing. If you would not say it to or in front of your parent or child, do not say it at all. When in doubt, keep quiet.
- DO privately and clearly state, in a nice way, what truly annoys you, and do it immediately. Do not wait! Do not overreact.

Experts note that sexual harassment often starts in its milder forms and escalates because the harasser assumed there was no objection to the earlier behaviors. Thus, it is extremely important that people speak up early.

Addressing Conflict

People seldom receive coaching or training on how to address conflict. Here are some suggestions. When you speak up:

- Use "I" messages, such as "I feel uncomfortable when… ."
- Avoid making smart remarks or quips.
- Be ready for some response, possibly even anger.
- Be prepared to tell the person what you want or need in order to keep a good relationship.
- If this is not the first occurrence, explain why you said nothing previously; for example, "I didn't want to offend you…."
- Be prepared to listen to the other person's side.

Adhering to these guidelines is of paramount importance when the person you are addressing is a supervisor. Always concentrate on the *behavior* in question, not the person's character or personality.

This is not easy if you have never approached relationships in this manner before. Before you try it, you may want to practice in front of the mirror or with friends.

A private written note, repeating what was stated earlier in conversation, may be appropriate. Privacy is important at this stage. Then, if the inappropriate behavior ceases, the relationship can continue positively.

DO YOU WORK IN A POSITIVE ENVIRONMENT?

The following self-test will help you evaluate your work environment, which may give you insights into areas that need improvement. If you are like most people, a lot of how you feel about work is based on only a few things:

- Whether you like the work itself
- How well you get along with the people
- Whether you think you are making a contribution

1. Of these factors, which is most important to you?

____

2. What do you do daily at work to make the environment positive?

____

____

3. List the positive qualities in your own work environment.

____

____

____

4. List what is missing for you in your work environment.

____

____

____

5. Do the positives outweigh what is missing?

____

____

CONTINUED

CONTINUED

6. If not, why are you working there?

7. On an average day, what percentage of your time at work is enjoyable?

8. Look at the positives you listed and your "what's missing" list. Which list contains most of the interpersonal elements?

9. What behaviors, if any, have you engaged in at work that someone might consider sexual harassment?

If you do not know, find out at once!

Part Summary

- Safety and security are called *dissatisfiers*. If they are not present, then people complain and productivity drops. In addition to providing a harassment-free workplace for legal reasons, organizations must consider the costs of lost time and productivity.
- Anti-harassment training can build teamwork, teach people how to constructively resolve conflicts, and help people gain respect and understanding for one another.
- Two fundamentals of anti-harassment training are:
    - DON'T touch another person in any way unless he or she has given you permission to do so. Do not make remarks that could be construed as harassing. When in doubt, keep quiet.
    - DO privately and clearly state, in a nice way, what truly annoys you, and do it immediately. Do not wait! Do not overreact.
- When addressing conflict, always concentrate on the *behavior* in question, not the person's character or personality.

"I heard a wolf whistle from behind that monitor."

APPENDIX

Appendix to Part 1

Comments & Suggested Responses

Test Your Knowledge of Sexual Harassment

1. **False**. Sexual harassment is not an issue that concerns only one gender. Women and men have both been sexually harassed, and men have been sexually harassed by other men.
2. **False**. Although it is important that all employers have a policy that prohibits sexual harassment in the workplace and prescribes discipline for violations of the policy, an employer must take other steps to ensure that sexual harassment does not occur. These steps include training all employees about sexual harassment, having in place an internal grievance mechanism that processes charges of sexual harassment, and investigating all charges of sexual harassment.
3. **False**. People need to enjoy coming to work. Limiting relationships between employees will not free an organization of sexual harassment; it might just create a less-than-enjoyable place to be. An organization should ensure, however, that when supervisors and subordinates date each other, these relationships are free of sexual harassment. Your organization may want to consider implementing an affirmative action policy.
4. **False**. In 1986, the U.S. Supreme Court found sexual harassment based on the standard of an objective, gender-neutral reasonable person, but several federal appellate courts have interpreted that standard as applicable to the reasonable woman.
5. **False**. According to a number of surveys, although situations of *quid pro quo* sexual harassment occur often in the workplace, instances of harassment that create an abusive or hostile environment occur more frequently.
6. **False**. See number 4 above.
7. **True**. A court can award damages for back pay, emotional harm, punitive damages, and attorney fees to an injured employee in a sexual harassment case. There have been cases in which the courts have prohibited the employer from paying the damages because of the injurious acts of sexual harassment.

8. **True**. This is a really difficult question. The EEOC Guidelines on sexual harassment say that where "employment is given to an employee because of his/her submission to the employer's request for sexual favors, the employer may be held liable for unlawful sexual discrimination against other persons who were qualified for but denied the employment opportunity or benefit." At least one court has coined the phrase *ugly discrimination* in describing this situation. It is clear that sexual harassment adversely affects not only the harassed employee, but also others in the work area that are denied employment opportunities because of the harassment.
9. **False**.
10. **False**. Sexual harassment can be stopped if an organization takes a positive stand against it by:
    - Establishing a policy prohibiting sexual harassment in the workplace
    - Publishing and posting the policy
    - Training all employees—including upper management—about sexual harassment
    - Implementing a grievance procedure so that employees can resolve claims
    - Informing all employees that the organization will discipline employees found guilty of sexual harassment, and that disciplinary actions might include termination

What Actions Constitute Sexual Harassment?

1. **False**. Physical acts are only one form of sexual harassment. Jokes, comments, leers, and cartoons with sexual undertones may also be considered sexual harassment.
2. **True**. The U.S. Supreme Court has said that acts that create a hostile or offensive work environment may constitute sexual harassment. A cartoon with sexual undertones may be considered sexual harassment if it creates a hostile or offensive environment.
3. **False**. Under most circumstances, this will not be considered sexual harassment. It might, however, be considered discrimination on the basis of sex.
4. **True**. Actions by clients, customers, or other non-employees may constitute sexual harassment. The employer who knows of the actions and takes no steps to stop them may be found legally liable.
5. **False**. Sexual harassment is a very personal matter. If it is "unwelcome," then staring or leering could be considered sexual harassment.

6. **False**. Actions of this type may create a hostile or offensive work environment.
7. **False**. Unwelcome acts or acts committed without permission are the essence of sexual harassment.
8. **False**. Acts of sexual harassment affect not only the direct participants, but also others who may be denied employment opportunities or who work in the same area.
9. **True**. This is a *quid pro quo* situation.
10. **True**. This is true if the subordinate believes that rejection may result in adverse employment action.

Appendix to Part 3

Comments & Suggested Responses

Do You "Know It When You See It"?

1. This is a classic example of harassment.
2. This is more complex. If the women consider this behavior harassing, the organization should protect itself by dealing with it.
3. This is even more complex. It addresses the question of whether a woman is responsible for comments that anyone makes about her when she wears suggestive clothing. Certainly if she considers the men's comments as sexually harassing, this is an incident of harassment. A workplace can head off this kind of problem by setting acceptable standards of dress. It is appropriate for her manager to discuss with her what is considered appropriate attire for work. This should have been done before the harassment occurred.
4. In most workplaces, calendars of nudes are inappropriate. The manager should talk to the individual about this and see that he removes the calendar.
5. This is another classic boss/subordinate case. The sex of the persons involved is irrelevant. If the man thinks that his female boss is harassing him, she is. It would be appropriate for him to tell her that he feels uncomfortable with the situation and that he thinks it is inappropriate for a work relationship. Because she is his boss, he must approach this discussion very carefully.
6. This situation is not uncommon. The lunch, although occurring away from the workplace, is an extension of work. Jokes with sexual overtones are not appropriate unless you are certain that no one will be offended. When the employee expressed offense at the joke, she should not have been told she was too sensitive. This situation could be the beginning of a claim of a hostile work environment if it is not dealt with immediately.
7. This situation is an example of a circumstance in which an employer could be liable for the harassing behavior of a client. Because the individual is a major client, this is a very sensitive situation.
8. This is not a case of sexual harassment. Nevertheless, such a case would have to be investigated in much the same manner, comparing performances of the individuals involved.

Case Study: Harassment in the Warehouse?

This is a case of discrimination and harassment, but not sexual harassment. It demonstrates one of the advantages of having an overall policy that covers all forms of harassment rather than one that covers only sexual harassment.

Alex Jordan will need to talk to Josh Strong and tell him emphatically that his behavior is not acceptable and must cease. If the company has a strong policy, this will be easier because Alex can quote the company policy. Alex should first give an oral warning and back it up with documentation in Josh's file. If Josh does not stop, Alex will need to give him a written warning and explain that unless this behavior ceases, he may be terminated. Once again, a policy backed up by a procedure provides the company with a much stronger case.

Because the problem is apparently spreading, Alex should meet with all of his employees in appropriate groups to discuss the company's stance on harassment, as well as the legal issues involved. Before he does this, Alex should consult Human Resources for guidance. Alex should document everything he does.

NOTE: Discrimination against homosexuals is not prohibited by federal law or the EEOC guidelines, but some states, counties, and municipalities do have such laws. Regardless, sexual harassment against homosexuals is not permitted.

Case Study: Salma and the VP

The first thing to do is to provide Salma with a safe place to talk and to vent her feelings. She is probably angry, hurt, and afraid. Discuss alternatives with Salma.

One alternative would be for Salma to approach the vice president and explain to him that she does not believe in mixing work and social relationships. This may require considerable coaching and some role-playing. Show Salma how she can remain polite while refusing his advances.

She might say, for example, "Mr. Smith, I am flattered by your asking me out. But I have a strong belief against mixing social and work relationships. This has nothing to do with you personally. I trust you will understand. I love my job and feel I am making a real contribution here."

Advise Salma to be prepared for some anger. Ask her to report the results to you.

Of course, if the vice president has seen her go out with anyone else from work, Salma will have to change her tactics. She will not be able to use separation of social and work relationships as a reason.

NOTE: This identical situation could easily occur if the sexes of the individuals are reversed or if the persons are of the same sex.

Another alternative would be to handle the matter yourself, if you are the appropriate person in your organization. If you are not, you can refer Salma to Human Resources. The complaint should be handled using the investigative procedures suggested in this book.

If Salma chooses to handle the situation herself first, she will need support and encouragement. If her attempts fail, the situation must be investigated.

Case Study: Heather Requests Privacy

Because of the manner in which the agencies and courts have interpreted the EEOC Guidelines, you have a responsibility to report the situation even if the employee requests that you do nothing. If, as a supervisor, you know about harassment and take no remedial steps, the organization can be found legally liable. If you are the Human Resources manager and you do nothing, the courts will not understand your lack of action. Once you, as a manager, know about the situation, it must be investigated, and if the facts show that sexual harassment is occurring, remedial steps must be taken.

Therefore, you would have to tell Heather that, although you understand her privacy concerns, you have an obligation to act. You should explain:

- Legal concerns
- That others may be affected
- That, unstopped, sexual harassment can spread and more broadly infect the workplace

Appendix to Part 5

Comments & Suggested Responses

Sample Agreement

NOTE: What follows is an example of a broad settlement document that an employer may use to ensure that all possible claims of the employee, such as possible tort and contract claims, are resolved.

1. The Organization shall pay Employee the gross sum of $___________ (less all normal and usual deductions for taxes and benefits) in settlement of any and all potential claims Employee believes he/she may have against the Organization. If Employee has revoked the waiver and release of all rights to proceed against the Organization, this Agreement may be nullified at the option of the Organization and no money will be paid.
2. [This section should include details about the payment by the Organization and other agreements by the Organization.]
3. This SETTLEMENT AGREEMENT AND GENERAL RELEASE is not and shall not in any way be construed as an admission by the Organization or any of its current or former employees of any wrongful acts or of any breach of any agreement whatsoever. The parties have entered into this SETTLEMENT AGREEMENT AND GENERAL RELEASE for the sole purpose of resolving all claims that the Employee may have against the Organization in order to avoid the burden, expense, delay, and uncertainties of litigation.
4. In consideration of the agreements and promises made by the Organization to Employee set forth in Paragraphs 1 and 2 above, Employee hereby releases the Organization and all of its current and former employees and agents from all claims (including those under Title VII of the Civil Rights Act of 1964, as amended), liabilities, obligations, promises, agreements, controversies, and damages of any nature and kind, known or unknown, attributable to or otherwise arising from any alleged conduct or practices by the Organization or any of its current or former employees or agents or otherwise related to Employee's employment relationship with the Organization or the termination thereof.

5. Employee further agrees, promises, and covenants that neither Employee nor any person acting on his/her behalf will file any action for damages or relief (including injunctive, declaratory, monetary relief, or other) against the Organization or any of its current or former employees or agents relating to any matter occurring in the past up to the date of this SETTLEMENT AGREEMENT AND GENERAL RELEASE or involving any continuing effects of actions and practices that arose before the date of this SETTLEMENT AGREEMENT AND RELEASE, or involving and based on any claims, demands, causes of action, obligations, damages, or liabilities that are the subject of this SETTLEMENT AGREEMENT AND GENERAL RELEASE.

6. Employee covenants and agrees to keep the terms, amount, and fact of the agreements set forth in this SETTLEMENT AGREEMENT AND GENERAL RELEASE completely confidential, and that Employee will never disclose any information concerning this SETTLEMENT AGREEMENT AND GENERAL RELEASE to any person other than his/her present attorneys.

7. Except as expressly provided below, neither Employee nor his/her representatives or attorneys shall make any statements to anyone (person, agency, entity, etc.) about the facts that relate to this settlement. If any person makes any inquiry of Employee, his/her attorneys, or any other representative of Employee that directly or indirectly relates to the Organization, then Employee, his/her attorneys, and representatives shall limit their response to a statement that all matters between Employee and the Organization have been resolved to the satisfaction of all parties. These provisions or restrictions shall not apply to any inquiry by a responsible governmental official or agency, nor shall they apply to any instance in which Employee is required to provide testimony or give evidence in response to a lawful order of a court of competent jurisdiction or an administrative body that has subpoena power. This confidentiality provision is hereby specifically identified as material to this SETTLEMENT AGREEMENT AND GENERAL RELEASE and it is specifically agreed that a breach of this term by Employee or his/her attorneys or representatives shall constitute a breach of this SETTLEMENT.

8. Employee represents and certifies that he/she has carefully read and fully understands all the provisions and effects of this SETTLEMENT AGREEMENT AND GENERAL RELEASE and has thoroughly discussed all aspects of this SETTLEMENT AGREEMENT AND GENERAL RELEASE with his/her private attorney, that Employee is voluntarily entering into this SETTLEMENT AGREEMENT AND GENERAL RELEASE, and that neither the Organization nor its agents, representatives, or attorneys made any representations about the terms of effects of this SETTLEMENT AGREEMENT AND GENERAL RELEASE other than those contained herein in writing.

9. Should any provision of this SETTLEMENT AGREEMENT AND GENERAL RELEASE be declared or be determined by any Court to be illegal or invalid, the validity of the remaining parts, terms, or provisions shall not be affected thereby, and said illegal or invalid part, term, or provision shall be deemed not part of this SETTLEMENT AGREEMENT AND GENERAL RELEASE.

10. This SETTLEMENT AGREEMENT AND GENERAL RELEASE sets forth the entire Agreement between the parties involved and fully supersedes any and all prior agreements or understandings between these parties pertaining to this subject matter.

11. Employee understands and agrees that this SETTLEMENT AGREEMENT AND GENERAL RELEASE shall bind and benefit the heirs, employees, predecessors, subsidiaries, parents, agents, affiliates, attorneys, and representatives of Employee and the Organization.

12. Employee understands and acknowledges that he/she has the right to have an attorney of his/her choice review this SETTLEMENT AGREEMENT AND GENERAL RELEASE.

PLEASE READ CAREFULLY. THIS SETTLEMENT AGREEMENT AND GENERAL RELEASE INCLUDES A RELEASE OF ALL KNOWN AND UNKNOWN CLAIMS.

In WITNESS WHEREOF and intending to be legally bound hereby, Employee has executed the foregoing SETTLEMENT AGREEMENT AND GENERAL RELEASE.

Executed at ___________ and ______________ this _____ day of ___________

WITNESS: EMPLOYEE:

_________________________ ______________________________

NOTE: If the charge is not settled at this stage, it will go forward to an investigation.

Appendix to Part 6

Comments & Suggested Responses

Case Study: Tom, the Killjoy?

A harasser is a person who looks at relationships through a sexual filter. No one expects people not to notice one another—not to notice how people look and what sex they are. That would be impossible. But noticing and abusing are not the same thing.

As men and women, and as people of different ethnic origins, we are taught to be polite at work. We may be seething inside, but we say nothing. Sometimes we even smile and laugh and act as if nothing is wrong.

When we carry the politeness to this extreme, we are expecting the other person or persons to intuit that we do not like their behavior. It simply does not work that way, especially in the more subtle situation of sexual harassment. In this situation, everyone but Tom is happy with the work environment. Tom is miserable and it is beginning to affect everyone.

A poor solution: Tom might have stopped Sandra right in her tracks with some quick remark. But such a response might only escalate the situation and increase conflict. Sandra would think Tom was a jerk and tell everyone else. The entire department would be negatively affected.

An effective solution: Tom could politely tell Sandra that he appreciated her compliments, but they made him feel uncomfortable and he preferred that she not repeat them. He could add that he thinks certain kinds of behavior are inappropriate in the office. Later, he could approach Amiel, explaining that he feels like a spoil-sport mentioning the joke, but he believes such jokes are out of place in the office. He could request that Amiel not tell such jokes when he is around. To soften things, Tom could learn some jokes he thinks are appropriate.

What about Georgia? She can have a private talk with Tom, mention her observations, and listen to his response. She can coach Tom on how to handle the situation. She can ask Tom for suggestions to keep the department friendly, fun, and team spirited, and still meet his needs for more decorum.

Viva-Crisp 50-Minute
Titles in the Series

ISBN	Author	Title	YOP	Price
9788130918174	Gambino	**50 Minutes to Better Software Demos**: *Apply Your Sales Skills with Confidence*	2011	195.00
9788130918488	Bozek	**50 One-Minute Tips to Better Communications**: *Speak, Write and Present More Effectively, 3/e*	2011	250.00
9788130918211	Conlow & Watsabaugh	**Achieving Supervisory Excellence**: *Be the Leader Your People Need*	2011	195.00
9788130918396	McKnight & Chapman	**Attitude**: *Protect Your Most Priceless Asset, 5/e*	2011	245.00
9788130918495	Terry Dickey	**Basics of Budgeting**: *Become a Better Business Planner, 2/e*	2011	250.00
9788130918310	Conlow & Watsabaugh	**Become a Successful Supervisor**: *Develop Essential People Skills*	2011	225.00
9788130918327	Brock	**Better Business Writing**: *Become A More Powerful Communicator, 5/e*	2011	225.00
9788130918228	Dupont	**Business Etiquette & Professionalism**: *Conduct Yourself With Confidence, 3/e*	2011	195.00
9788130918181	Morgan	**Calming Upset Customers**: *Stay in Control ... In any Situation, 4/e*	2011	195.00
9788130918198	Minor	**Coaching and Counseling**: *Become a Better Manager Through Mentoring, 4/e*	2011	195.00
9788130918273	Decker	**Communication Skills for Leaders**: *Deliver a Clear and Consistent Message, 4/e*	2011	225.00
9788130918143	Kindler	**Conflict Management**: *Resolve Disagreement at Work, 4/e*	2011	165.00
9788130918280	Conlow & Watsabaugh	**Creating a High Performance Team**: *Gain the Skills of Today's Successful Leaders*	2011	225.00
9788130918334	Feldman	**Critical Thinking**: *Make Strategic Decisions With Confidence, 2/e*	2011	225.00
9788130918426	Flynn	**E-Mail Management**: *Keep Your Inbox Under Control, 2/e*	2011	245.00
9788130918471	Kravitz & Schubert	**Emotional Intelligence Works**: *Think, Be and Work Smarter, 3/e*	2011	245.00
9788130918150	Maddux	**Ethics in Business**: *Manage With Authority and Fairness, 2/e*	2011	195.00
9788130918235	Rouillard	**Goals and Goal Setting**: *Achieve Measurable Results, 4/e*	2011	195.00
9788130918204	Conlow Watsabaugh	**Handling Difficult People and Situations**: *Lead People Through Adversity*	2011	195.00

ISBN	Author	Title	YOP	Price
9788130918433	Wendover	**High Performance Hiring**: *Select the Best Every Time, 3/e*	2011	245.00
9788130918402	Shea	**Making the Most of Being Mentored**: *Mentors Help Mentees Do, 2/e*	2011	245.00
9788130918242	Scott	**Managing Personal Change**: *Stay Positive and Stay in Control*, 3/e	2011	195.00
9788130918341	Haynes	**Meeting Skills for Leaders**: *Make Meetings More Productive, 4/e*	2011	225.00
9788130918440	Shea	**Mentoring**: *Make It A Mutually Rewarding Experience, 4/e*	2011	245.00
9788130918525	Shandler	**Motivating the Millennial Knowledge Worker**: *Help Today's Workforce Succeed in Today's Economy*	2011	395.00
9788130918167	Mandel	**Presentation Skills**: *Captivate and Educate Your Audience, 4/e*	2011	195.00
9788130918518	Pokras	**Problem Solving for Teams**: *Make Consensus More Achievable, 3/e*	2011	295.00
9788130918259	Haynes	**Project Management**: *Get from the Idea to Implementation Successfully, 4/e*	2011	195.00
9788130918372	Martin	**Quality Customer Service**: *Satisfy Customers– It's Everybody's Job, 5/e*	2011	245.00
9788130918457	Lightle & Doucet	**Sexual Harassment in the Workplace**: *Create a Better Workplace For Everyone, 3/e*	2011	245.00
9788130918501	Lengefeld	**Study Skills Strategies**: *Get the Most From Every Minute of Learning, 4/e*	2011	250.00
9788130918358	Conlow & Watsabaugh	**SuperSTAR Customer Service**: *It's all about C.A.R.E.*	2011	225.00
9788130918297	Maddux & Wingfield	**Team Building**: *Turn Personal Strengths Into Group Success, 5/e*	2011	225.00
9788130918464	Finch	**Telephone Courtesy & Customer Service**: *Be Your Company's Lifeline to Customers, 4/e*	2011	245.00
9788130918389	Conlow & Watsabaugh	**Telephone Skills that Satisfy Customers**: *Unleash the Full Potential of the Telephone*	2011	245.00
9788130918303	Romero	**The Business of Listening**: *Become a More Effective Listener, 4/e*	2011	225.00
9788130918365	Chapman & McKnight	**The New Supervisor**: *Lead With Confidence, 5/e*	2011	225.00
9788130918266	Haynes	**Time Management**: *Get An Extra Day a Week*	2011	195.00
9788130918419	Gill & Chatton	**Understanding Financial Statements**: *Master the Tools That Help You Succeed, 3/e*	2011	245.00